Miss Rosie's
-quilt collection-

If you adore quilts in harmonious colors, then you must have this collection of patterns from Carrie Nelson! Choose the antique tones of Radio Flyer and zip through your quilt's creation. Or stop and smell the pastel flowers while piecing Rosie's Posies. For quilts that make your heart sing, stitch Amadeus in rich, lively shades and Uptown Girl in fun, refreshing hues. Read Carrie's helpful tips to fashion all fourteen of these precisely pieced, machine-quilted beauties. You deserve the happiness of making quilts like these!

LEISURE ARTS, INC.
Little Rock, Arkansas

Amadeus

Finished Quilt Size: 72¹/₂" x 72¹/₂" (184 cm x 184 cm)
Finished Block Size: 12" x 12" (30 cm x 30 cm)

Pieced by Carrie Nelson.
Quilted by Louise Haley.

Five color groups and lots of prints make the Amadeus quilt "music to the eyes." Whether you make your quilt with 5 prints or 35, the composition is still pretty simple. Just 25 star blocks and a pieced border! Follow the music, or find your own tune (your own colors), and play along.

The name is in honor of Wolfgang Amadeus Mozart, a favorite composer of Carrie's Uncle Harry. (Another favorite of Harry's is Beethoven, but Carrie didn't think "Ludwig" was a name she wanted to give her quilt.)

YARDAGE REQUIREMENTS

*Yardage is based on 43"/44"
(109 cm/112 cm) wide fabric with
a "usable" width of 40" (102 cm) after
trimming selvages and shrinkage. Yardage
requirements may vary depending on number
of prints used.*

$1^1/_2$ yds (1.4 m) *total* of assorted
yellow print fabrics

$2^7/_8$ yds (2.6 m) *total* of assorted
beige print fabrics

$1^1/_2$ yds (1.4 m) *total* of assorted red
print fabrics

$1^3/_4$ yds (1.6 m) *total* of assorted
blue print fabrics

$1^3/_4$ yds (1.6 m) *total* of assorted
green print fabrics

*6$^3/_4$ yds (6.2 m) of fabric for
backing

$^7/_8$ yd (80 cm) of fabric for binding

You will also need:

81" x 81" (206 cm x 206 cm) square
of batting

*Yardage is based on 3 lengths of
fabric, which allows for a larger
backing for long arm quilting. If
you are using another quilting
method, 2 lengths, or 4$^1/_2$ yds
(4.1 m), will be adequate.

CUTTING OUT THE PIECES

*Follow **Rotary Cutting**, page 103, to cut
fabric. All measurements include $^1/_4$" seam
allowances.*

For *each* of 7 Block A's:

- Cut 1 **large square** $6^1/_2$" x $6^1/_2$"
  from yellow print.
- Cut 4 **sew and flip squares**
  $3^1/_2$" x $3^1/_2$" from 1 green print.
- Cut 4 **rectangles** $6^1/_2$" x $3^1/_2$"
  from 1 beige print.
- Cut 8 **star point squares**
  $3^1/_2$" x $3^1/_2$" from 1 red print.
- Cut 4 **corner squares** $3^1/_2$" x $3^1/_2$"
  from 1 blue print.

For *each* of 6 Block B's:

- Cut 1 **large square** $6^1/_2$" x $6^1/_2$" from yellow print.
- Cut 4 **sew and flip squares** $3^1/_2$" x $3^1/_2$" from
  1 blue print.
- Cut 4 **rectangles** $6^1/_2$" x $3^1/_2$" from 1 beige print.
- Cut 8 **star point squares** $3^1/_2$" x $3^1/_2$" from 1 red print.
- Cut 4 **corner squares** $3^1/_2$" x $3^1/_2$" from 1 green print.

For *each* of 6 Block C's:

- Cut 1 **large square** $6^1/_2$" x $6^1/_2$" from yellow print.
- Cut 4 **sew and flip squares** $3^1/_2$" x $3^1/_2$" from
  1 red print.
- Cut 4 **rectangles** $6^1/_2$" x $3^1/_2$" from 1 beige print.
- Cut 8 **star point squares** $3^1/_2$" x $3^1/_2$" from
  1 blue print.
- Cut 4 **corner squares** $3^1/_2$" x $3^1/_2$" from 1 beige print.

For *each* of 6 Block D's:

- Cut 1 **large square** $6^1/_2$" x $6^1/_2$" from yellow print.
- Cut 4 **sew and flip squares** $3^1/_2$" x $3^1/_2$" from
  1 red print.
- Cut 4 **rectangles** $6^1/_2$" x $3^1/_2$" from 1 beige print.
- Cut 8 **star point squares** $3^1/_2$" x $3^1/_2$" from
  1 green print.
- Cut 4 **corner squares** $3^1/_2$" x $3^1/_2$" from 1 beige print.

For pieced borders:

- Cut 10 squares $7^1/_4$" x $7^1/_4$" from assorted yellow
  prints. Cut squares *twice* diagonally to make
  40 **small triangles**.
- Cut 10 squares $7^1/_4$" x $7^1/_4$" from assorted beige
  prints. Cut squares *twice* diagonally to make
  40 **small triangles**.
- Cut 12 squares $6^7/_8$" x $6^7/_8$" from assorted blue
  prints. Cut squares *once* diagonally to make
  24 **large triangles**.
- Cut 12 squares $6^7/_8$" x $6^7/_8$" from assorted green
  prints. Cut squares *once* diagonally to make
  24 **large triangles**.

MAKING THE BLOCKS

*Follow **Piecing**, page 103, and **Pressing**, page 104. Use ¹/₄" seam allowances throughout.*

Block A

1. With right sides together, place 1 green **sew and flip square** on 1 corner of yellow **large square** and stitch diagonally. Trim ¹/₄" from stitching line (**Fig. 1**). Open up and press seam allowances toward triangle (**Fig. 2**).

Fig. 1

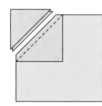

Fig. 2

2. Continue adding green **sew and flip squares** to corners of **large square** as shown in **Fig. 3**, pressing seam allowances toward triangles, to make **Unit 1**.

Fig. 3

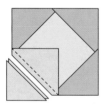

Unit 1

3. With right sides together, place 1 red **star point square** on 1 end of 1 beige **rectangle** and stitch diagonally. Trim ¹/₄" from stitching line (**Fig. 4**). Open up and press seam allowances toward triangle (**Fig. 5**).

Fig. 4

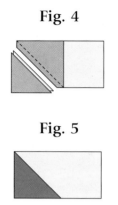

Fig. 5

4. Place another red **star point square** on opposite end of **rectangle**. Stitch and trim as shown in **Fig. 6**. Open up and press seam allowances toward triangle to make **Flying Geese Unit**. Make 4 **Flying Geese Units**.

Fig. 6

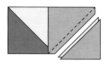

Flying Geese Unit (make 4)

*Before going further, read **A Note from Carrie About Pressing**, page 7.*

5. Sew 2 blue **corner squares** and 1 **Flying Geese Unit** together to make **Unit 2**. Make 2 **Unit 2's**.

Unit 2 (make 2)

About Pressing: ✍

A Note from Carrie

I have found that for many blocks, pressing the seams open yields the best results. Most of us learn that seams are never pressed open; they are always pressed to one side. However, that "school of thought" seems to be changing. Most of the recent commentary on the subject in books and magazines, on televised quilting shows and from nationally recognized quilting teachers is that the reasons for pressing seams to one side no longer apply. The fabrics that we use today are better, as is the quality of thread and batting, and since most of us use sewing machines, our stitches are smaller and tighter. Consequently, we have fewer concerns about any problems that might arise when seams are pressed open. And simply put, I have found that – for me – the results are worth it as points are sharper and seams are flatter. But in the end, it is entirely a personal choice.

If you plan to quilt in the ditch, you should press seam allowances to one side. If pressing seam allowances to one side, follow these diagrams.

Blocks with red points   Blocks with blue or green points

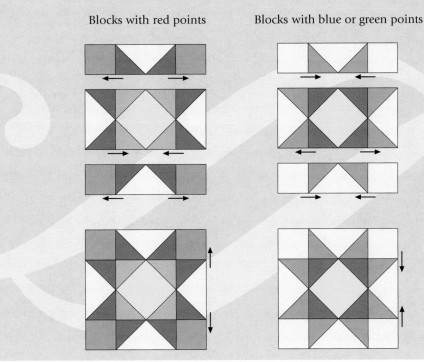

---

6. Sew 2 **Flying Geese Units** and **Unit 1** together to make **Unit 3**.

Unit 3

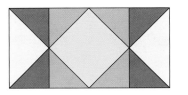

7. Sew 2 **Unit 2's** and **Unit 3** together to make **Block A**.

Block A

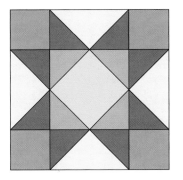

8. Repeat Steps 1 – 7 to make 7 **Block A's**.

9. Repeat Steps 1 – 7 using yellow **large square**, blue **sew and flip squares**, beige **rectangles**, red **star point squares**, and green **corner squares** to make 6 **Block B's**.

Block B (make 6)

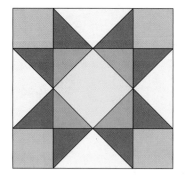

10. Repeat Steps 1 – 7 using yellow **large square**, red **sew and flip squares**, beige **rectangles**, blue **star point squares**, and beige **corner squares** to make 6 **Block C's**.

Block C (make 6)

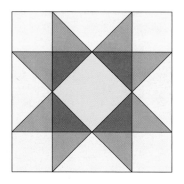

11. Repeat Steps 1 – 7 using yellow **large square**, red **sew and flip squares**, beige **rectangles**, green **star point squares**, and beige **corner squares** to make 6 **Block D's**.

Block D (make 6)

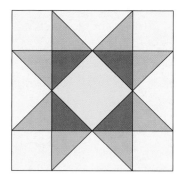

ASSEMBLING THE QUILT TOP CENTER

*Refer to **Quilt Top Diagram**, page 9, for placement.*

1. Sew **Blocks** together in this order (*left to right*): A, D, B, D, A to make **Row 1**. Repeat to make **Row 5**.
2. Sew **Blocks** together in this order (*left to right*): C, B, C, B, C to make **Row 2**. Repeat to make **Row 4**.
3. Sew **Blocks** together in this order (*left to right*): A, D, A, D, A to make **Row 3**.
4. Sew **Rows** together to complete quilt top center.

ADDING THE BORDERS

1. Sew 1 yellow **small triangle** and 1 beige **small triangle** together as shown to make 20 **Unit 4a's** and 20 **Unit 4b's**.

Unit 4a (make 20)   **Unit 4b** (make 20)

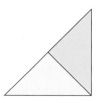   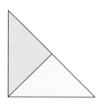

Sew 1 blue **large triangle** and 1 **Unit 4a** together to make **Unit 5a**. Make 20 **Unit 5a's**.

Unit 5a (make 20)

Sew 1 green **large triangle** and 1 **Unit 4b** together to make **Unit 5b**. Make 20 **Unit 5b's**.

Unit 5b (make 20)

Sew 1 **Unit 5a** and 1 **Unit 5b** together to make **Border Unit**. Make 20 **Border Units**.

Border Unit (make 20)

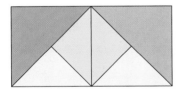

Sew 1 blue **large triangle** and 1 green **large triangle** together to make **Corner Border Unit**. Make 4 **Corner Border Units**.

Corner Border Unit (make 4)

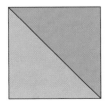

6. Sew 5 **Border Units** together end to end to make **border**. Make 4 **borders**.

Border (make 4)

7. Sew 1 **Corner Border Unit** to *each* end of **top** and **bottom borders**.
8. Matching centers and corners and easing any fullness, sew **side borders** to quilt top center.
9. Matching centers and corners and easing any fullness, sew **top/bottom borders** to quilt top.

COMPLETING THE QUILT

1. Follow **Quilting**, page 105, to mark, layer, and quilt as desired. *(**Note**: Stay-stitching around the quilt top approximately $1/8$" from the edge before quilting will help stabilize the edge and prevent any seams from separating.)* Our quilt is machine quilted with feather patterns and outline quilting.
2. Cut a 27" square of binding fabric. Follow **Binding**, page 108, to bind quilt using 2"w bias binding with mitered corners.

Quilt Top Diagram

9

Tag Sale

Finished Quilt Size: 80$\frac{1}{2}$" x 80$\frac{1}{2}$" (204 cm x 204 cm)
Finished Block Size: 7$\frac{1}{2}$" x 7$\frac{1}{2}$" (19 cm x 19 cm)

Pieced by Carrie Nelson.
Quilted by Darlene Johannis.

We all know at least one of "them" — those tag-, garage-, yard-sale queens who go rooting through dilapidated boxes and digging through piles of ratty old blankets to find a wonderful antique quilt that has never been washed … and then they pay $10.00 for it. Since most of us aren't that lucky (or determined), Carrie created this "shabby chic" quilt from beautiful new fabrics.

Made the old-fashioned way (without strip sets), "Tag Sale" is totally scrappy for a truly vintage look and feel.

Tip: Our quilt has only 4 **Simple Star Blocks** scattered throughout the quilt top. To include more, cut fewer pieces for the **Large Nine-Patch Blocks** and more pieces for the **Simple Star Blocks**. You will need to cut a total of 40 of these 2 Blocks and 41 **Small Nine-Patch Blocks**.

YARDAGE REQUIREMENTS

Yardage is based on 43"/44" (109 cm/112 cm) wide fabric with a "usable" width of 40" (102 cm) after trimming selvages and shrinkage.

$7^3/_8$ yds (6.7 m) *total* of assorted pastel print fabrics
$^1/_2$ yd (46 m) of cream print fabric for inner borders
$7^1/_2$ yds (6.9 m) of fabric for backing
$^7/_8$ yd (80 cm) of fabric for binding

You will also need:

89" x 89" (226 cm x 226 cm) square of batting

CUTTING OUT THE PIECES

*Follow **Rotary Cutting**, page 103, to cut fabric. All strips are cut across the width of the fabric unless otherwise noted. All measurements include $^1/_4$" seam allowances. Each "set" should be cut from 1 fabric or similar color fabrics.*

From assorted pastel print fabrics:

For Small Nine-Patch Blocks
- Cut 41 sets of 5 **square A's** $2^1/_4$" x $2^1/_4$".
- Cut 41 sets of 4 **square B's** $2^1/_4$" x $2^1/_4$".
- Cut 41 sets of 4 **triangle C's**. For each set, cut 2 squares $4^5/_8$" x $4^5/_8$". Cut squares *once* diagonally to make 4 **triangle C's**.

For Large Nine-Patch Blocks
- Cut 36 sets of 5 **square D's** 3" x 3".
- Cut 36 sets of 4 **square E's** 3" x 3".

For Simple Star Blocks
- Cut 4 sets of 8 **square F's** 3" x 3".
- Cut 4 sets of 1 **square G** 3" x 3" and 8 **square H's** $1^3/_4$" x $1^3/_4$".

For Outer Border
- Cut 56 **large border squares** $5^1/_2$" x $5^1/_2$".
- Cut 16 **small border squares** 3" x 3".

From cream print fabric:
- Cut 8 **border strips** $1^3/_4$"w.

MAKING THE BLOCKS

*Before sewing, organize all **Blocks** into desired color combinations. Follow **Piecing**, page 103, and **Pressing**, page 104, to assemble the quilt top. Use $^1/_4$" seam allowances throughout.*

Small Nine-Patch Blocks

1. Sew 2 **square A's** and 1 **square B** together to make **Unit 1**. Press seam allowances toward **square A's**. Make 2 **Unit 1's**.

Unit 1 (make 2)

2. Sew 2 **square B's** and 1 **square A** together to make **Unit 2**. Press seam allowances toward **square A**.

Unit 2

3. Sew 2 **Unit 1's** and **Unit 2** together to make **Unit 3**. Press seam allowances toward **Unit 1's**.

Unit 3

4. Sew **Unit 3** and 4 **triangle C's** together to make **Small Nine-Patch Block**. Press seam allowances toward **triangle C's**.

Small Nine-Patch Block

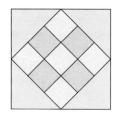

5. Repeat Steps 1 – 4 to make 41 **Small Nine-Patch Blocks**.

Large Nine-Patch Blocks

1. Sew 2 **square D's** and 1 **square E** together to make **Unit 4**. Press seam allowances toward **square D's**. Make 2 **Unit 4's**.

Unit 4 (make 2)

2. Sew 2 **square E's** and 1 **square D** together to make **Unit 5**. Press seam allowances toward **square D**.

Unit 5

3. Sew 2 **Unit 4's** and **Unit 5** together to make **Large Nine-Patch Block**. Press seam allowances toward **Unit 4's**.

Large Nine-Patch Block

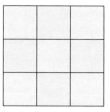

4. Repeat Steps 1 – 3 to make 36 **Large Nine-Patch Blocks**.

Simple Star Blocks

1. With right sides together, place 1 **square H** on 1 corner of 1 **square F** and stitch diagonally (**Fig. 1**). Trim ¼" from stitching line (**Fig. 2**). Open up and press seam allowances toward triangle.

Fig. 1

Fig. 2

Add a second **square H** to adjacent corner of **square F** as shown in **Fig. 3**. Open up and press seam allowances toward triangle to complete **Unit 6**. Make 4 **Unit 6's**.

Fig. 3

Unit 6 (make 4)

Sew 2 **square F's** and 1 **Unit 6** together to make **Unit 7**. Press seam allowances toward **square F's**. Make 2 **Unit 7's**.

Unit 7 (make 2)

Sew 2 **Unit 6's** and **square G** together to make **Unit 8**. Press seam allowances toward **square G**.

Unit 8

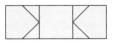

5. Sew 2 **Unit 7's** and **Unit 8** together to make **Simple Star Block**. Press seam allowances toward **Unit 8**.

Simple Star Block

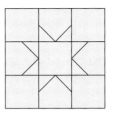

6. Repeat Steps 1 – 5 to make 4 **Simple Star Blocks**.

ASSEMBLING THE QUILT TOP CENTER
*Refer to **Quilt Top Diagram**, page 17, for placement.*

1. Arrange **Blocks** on floor or design wall in a manner pleasing to you. Alternate **Small Nine-Patch Blocks** with **Large Nine-Patch Blocks** and **Simple Star Blocks** in horizontal **Rows** of 9 **Blocks**. Press seam allowances toward **Large Nine-Patch** or **Simple Star Blocks**.
2. Sew horizontal **Rows** together to complete quilt top center. Press seam allowances in one direction.

ADDING THE BORDERS

1. Using diagonal seams, sew **border strips** together end to end (**Fig. 4**) to make 1 continuous **inner border strip**.

Fig. 4

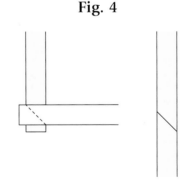

2. From **inner border strip**, cut 4 **inner borders** 74½"l.
3. Mark the center of each edge of quilt top. Mark the center of each **inner border**. Measure across center of quilt top. Beginning at center of **top inner border**, measure ½ the width of the quilt top in both directions and mark.
4. Matching raw edges and marks on **top inner border** with center and corners of quilt top and easing in any fullness, pin **top inner border** to quilt top. Sew **top inner border** to quilt top, beginning and ending exactly ¼" from each corner of quilt top. Backstitch at beginning and ending of stitching to reinforce.
5. Repeat Steps 3 – 4 to sew **bottom** and then **side inner borders** to quilt top.
6. Fold 1 corner of quilt top diagonally with right sides together and matching edges. Aligning ruler with fold, use ruler to mark stitching line as shown in **Fig. 5**. Sew on drawn line, backstitching at beginning and ending of stitching. Turn mitered corner right side up. Check to make sure corner will lie flat with no gaps or puckers. Trim seam allowances to ¼" and press to one side. Repeat for other corners.

Fig. 5

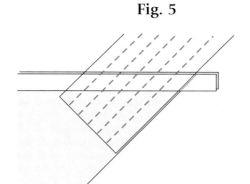

7. In random color order, sew 14 **large border squares** together end to end to make 1 **outer border**. Make 4 **outer borders**. Press seam allowances in one direction.
8. Sew 4 **small border squares** together to make **Corner Unit**. Make 4 **Corner Units**.

Corner Unit (make 4)

9. Sew 1 **corner unit** to each end of 2 **outer borders** to make **top/bottom outer borders**. Press seam allowances toward **Corner Units**.
10. Matching centers and corners and easing any fullness, sew **side**, **top**, and then **bottom outer borders** to quilt top. Press seam allowances toward **inner borders**.

COMPLETING THE QUILT

- Follow **Quilting**, page 105, to mark, layer, and quilt as desired. (*Note: Stay-stitching around the quilt top approximately ¹/₈" from the edge before quilting will help stabilize the edge and prevent any seams from separating.*) Our quilt is free-motion machine quilted with a swirl pattern.
- Cut a 28" square of binding fabric. Follow **Binding**, page 108, to bind quilt using 2"w bias binding with mitered corners.

Quilt Top Diagram

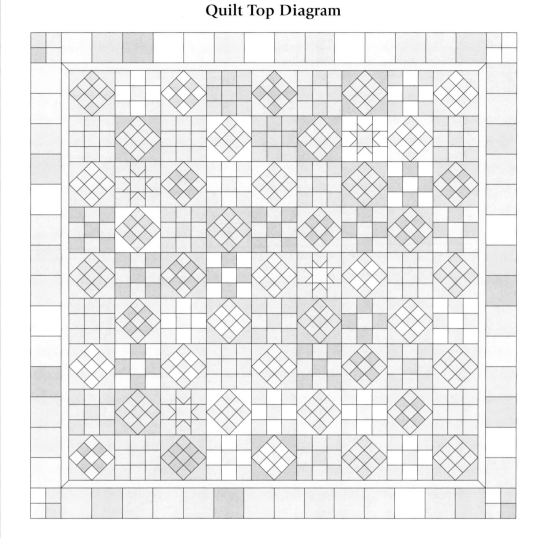

Grandma's Scrap Bag

Finished Quilt Size: 76^1/$_2$" x 87" (194 cm x 221 cm)
Finished Block Size: 7^1/$_2$" x 7^1/$_2$" (19 cm x 19 cm)

Pieced by Sue Maitre.
Quilted by Louise Haley.

While Carrie's grandmother wasn't a quilter, she did have a scrap bag (actually, it was a basket) of fabrics leftover from her sewing projects. If she had made a quilt from her scraps, supposes Carrie, it would have looked a lot like this one.

There are 1,143 pieces in this quilt, making it a perfect project to empty your own scrap bag!

YARDAGE REQUIREMENTS

Yardage is based on 43"/44" (109 cm/112 cm) wide fabric with a "usable" width of 40" (102 cm) after trimming selvages and shrinkage.

$4^7/_8$ yds (4.5 m) *total of assorted print fabrics*

$4^1/_4$ yds (3.9 m) of cream print fabric

$7^1/_8$ yds (6.5 m) of fabric for backing

You will also need:

85" x 95" (216 cm x 241 cm) rectangle of batting

CUTTING OUT THE PIECES

*Follow **Rotary Cutting**, page 103, to cut fabric. All strips are cut across the width of the fabric unless otherwise noted. Borders include an extra 4" of length for "insurance" and will be trimmed after assembling quilt top center. All other measurements include $^1/_4$" seam allowances.*

From assorted print fabrics:

- Cut 42 sets of 4 matching **rectangles** 2" x $3^1/_2$".
- Cut 56 **medium squares** $2^5/_8$" x $2^5/_8$".
- Cut 42 **small squares** 2" x 2".
- Cut 100 **strips** 2" x 20".

Set aside left over assorted print fabrics for scrappy binding.

From cream print fabric:

- Cut 16 strips $3^1/_2$"w. From these strips, cut 168 **large squares** $3^1/_2$" x $3^1/_2$".
- Cut 2 *lengthwise* **side borders** $5^1/_2$" x 81".
- Cut 2 *lengthwise* **top/bottom borders** $5^1/_2$" x $80^1/_2$".

From remaining width:

- Cut 19 strips 3"w. From these strips, cut 112 squares 3" x 3". Cut squares *once* diagonally to make 224 **triangles**.

MAKING THE BLOCKS

*Follow **Piecing**, page 103, and **Pressing**, page 104, to assemble the quilt top. Use $^1/_4$" seam allowances throughout. For each **Block**, use 1 set of 4 matching **rectangles**.*

1. Sew 2 **large squares** and 1 **rectangle** together to make **Unit 1**. Press seam allowances toward **rectangle**. Make 2 matching **Unit 1's**.

Unit 1 (make 2)

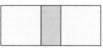

2. Sew 2 **rectangles** (which match **Unit 1's**) and 1 contrasting **small square** together to make **Unit 2**. Press seam allowances toward **rectangles**.

Unit 2

3. Sew 2 **Unit 1's** and **Unit 2** together to make **Block**. Press seam allowances toward **Unit 2**.

Block

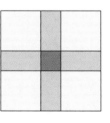

4. Repeat Steps 1 – 3 to make 42 **Blocks**

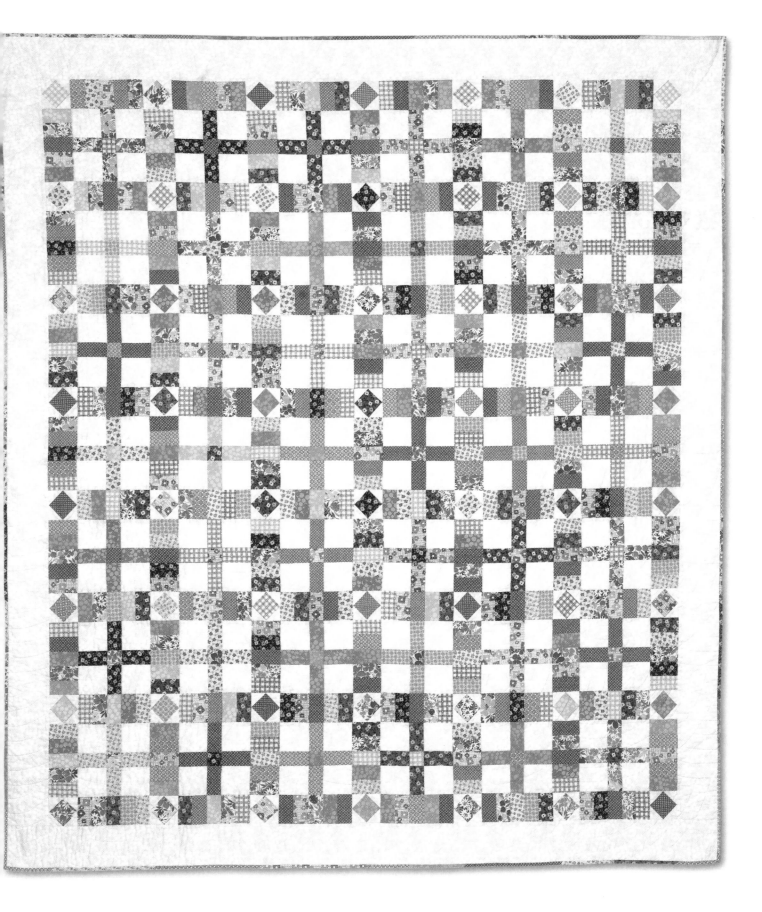

MAKING THE SASHING UNITS

1. Sew 5 **strips** together to make **Strip Set**. Press seam allowances away from middle **strip**. Make 20 **Strip Sets**. Cut across **Strip Sets** at $3^1/2$" intervals to make 97 **Unit 3's**.

Strip Set (make 20)

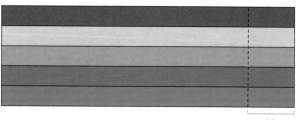

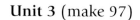

$3^1/2$"

Unit 3 (make 97)

2. Referring to **Fig. 1**, sew 4 **triangles** to sides of 1 **medium square** to make **Unit 4**. Press seam allowances toward **triangles**. Trim **Unit 4** to $3^1/2$" x $3^1/2$" (shown by red dashed line in **Fig. 2**). *Be sure there is a $1/4$" seam allowance at each point.* Make 56 **Unit 4's**.

Fig. 1

Fig. 2

Unit 4 (make 56)

ASSEMBLING THE QUILT TOP CENTER

1. Alternating **Unit 3's** and **Blocks**, sew 7 **Unit 3's** and 6 **Blocks** together to make **Row**. Press seam allowances toward **Unit 3's**. Make 7 **Rows**.

Row (make 7)

2. Alternating **Unit 4's** and **Unit 3's**, sew 7 **Unit 4's** and 6 **Unit 3's** together to make **Sashing Row**. Press seam allowances toward **Unit 3's**. Make 8 **Sashing Rows**.

Sashing Row (make 8)

3. Referring to **Quilt Top Diagram**, page 23, alternate and sew **Sashing Rows** and **Rows** together to make center section of quilt top. Press seam allowances toward **Rows**.

ADDING THE BORDERS

1. To determine length of **side borders**, measure *length* of quilt top center. Trim 2 **side borders** to determined length. Matching centers and corners sew **side borders** to quilt top.
2. To determine length of **top/bottom borders**, measure *width* of quilt top center (including added borders). Trim 2 **top/bottom borders** to determined length. Matching centers and corners, sew **top/bottom borders** to quilt top.

COMPLETING THE QUILT

- Follow **Quilting**, page 105, to mark, layer, and quilt as desired. Our quilt is machine quilted with a large Baptist Fan pattern.
- The scrappy binding is made using left over assorted print fabrics from the quilt top. Cut bias strips 2"w in various lengths and sew together using diagonal seams (**Fig. 3**) into a continuous strip 9½ yds long. Follow **Attaching Binding with Mitered Corners**, page 109, to bind quilt.

Fig. 3

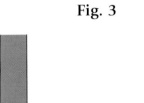

Quilt Top Diagram

Loose Change

Finished Quilt Size: 73¹/₂" x 81" (187 cm x 206 cm)
Finished Block Size: 5¹/₄" x 5¹/₄" (13 cm x 13 cm)

Pieced by Cheryl Jeffries.
Quilted by Darlene Johannis

Carrie says she's a sucker for a nine-patch quilt. "I think nine-patches are perfect. They're fast and they're easy to make. They can be made with two fabrics or with nine. Large or small, prints or plaids, straight setting or on point, anything works. And, the more of them you have, the better they look. To top it off, they're just so darn 'neat' looking."

As for the title, "It just seemed to fit."

Tip: The instructions for this quilt include short strip sets to make the blocks. If you have small scraps you want to use up, just cut nine squares 2 1/4" x 2 1/4" for each block. You may want to add a few of these scrappy blocks at random, or you can make all of the 128 blocks this way.

Follow the pressing suggestions to make piecing the quilt top a little easier.

YARDAGE REQUIREMENTS

Yardage is based on 43"/44" (109 cm/112 cm) wide fabric with a "usable" width of 40" (102 cm) after trimming selvages and shrinkage.

- 7 1/2 yds (6.9 m) *total* of assorted light, medium, and dark print fabrics
- 1 1/8 yds (1 m) of burgundy print fabric for setting triangles and borders
- 2 3/8 yds (2.2 m) of gold print fabric for borders
- *6 7/8 yds (6.3 m) of fabric for backing
- 7/8 yds (80 cm) of fabric for binding

You will also need:

- 82" x 89" (208 cm x 226 cm) rectangle of batting
- *Yardage is based on 3 lengths of fabric, which allows for a larger backing for long arm quilting. If you are using another quilting method, 2 lengths, or 5 yds (4.6 m), will be adequate.

CUTTING OUT THE PIECES

*Follow **Rotary Cutting**, page 103, to cut fabric. All strips are cut across the width of the fabric unless otherwise noted. Borders include an extra 4" of length for "insurance" and will be trimmed after assembling quilt top center. All other measurements include 1/4" seam allowances. Each "set" should be cut from 1 fabric or similar color fabrics.*

From assorted light, medium, and dark print fabrics:
- Cut 144 sets of 3 **strips** 2 1/4" x 10".

From burgundy print fabric:
- Cut 8 **border strips** 1 1/2"w.
- Cut 2 strips 8 3/4"w. From these strips, cut 8 squares 8 3/4" x 8 3/4". Cut squares *twice* diagonally to make 32 **setting triangles**. (You will use 30 **setting triangles** and have 2 left over.)
- Cut 2 squares 4 5/8" x 4 5/8". Cut squares *once* diagonally to make 4 **corner setting triangles**.

From gold print fabric:
- Cut 4 *lengthwise* **outer borders** 4 1/4" x 77 1/2".
- Cut 2 *lengthwise* **side inner borders** 2 1/4" x 72".
- Cut 2 *lengthwise* **top/bottom inner borders** 2 1/4" x 68".

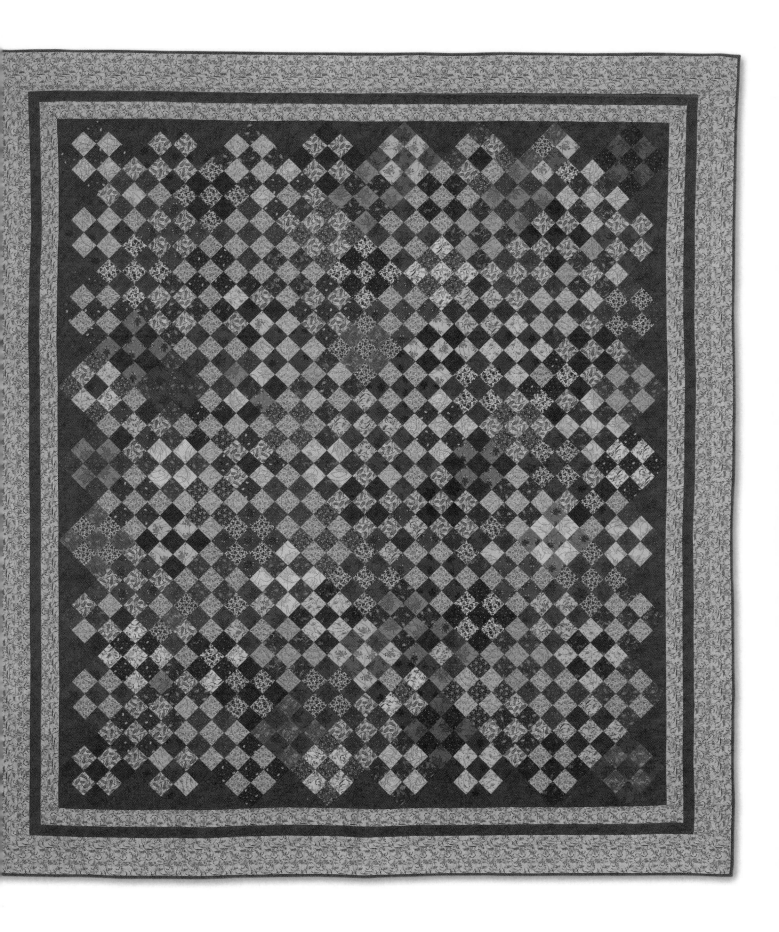

MAKING THE BLOCKS

*Follow **Piecing**, page 103, and **Pressing**, page 104, to assemble the quilt top. Use ¹/₄" seam allowances throughout.*

1. Select 2 contrasting sets of **strips**. Sew 2 **strips** from the first set and 1 **strip** from the second set together to make **Strip Set A**. Press seam allowances toward outer **strips**. Sew 2 **strips** from the second set and 1 **strip** from the first set to make **Strip Set B**. Press seam allowances toward middle **strip**. Cut across **Strip Set A** at 2¹/₄" intervals to make 3 **Unit 1's**. Cut across **Strip Set B** at 2¹/₄" intervals to make 3 **Unit 2's**.

Strip Set A **Unit 1** (make 3)

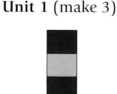
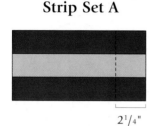

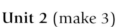

2¹/₄"

Strip Set B **Unit 2** (make 3)

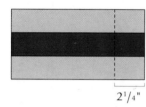

2¹/₄"

2. Sew 2 **Unit 1's** and 1 **Unit 2** together to make **Block A**. Press seam allowances toward **Unit 1's**. Sew 2 **Unit 2's** and 1 **Unit 1** together to make **Block B**. Press seam allowances toward **Unit 1**.

Block A **Block B**

3. Repeat Steps 1 – 2 to make 72 **Block A's** and 56 **Block B's**.

ASSEMBLING THE QUILT TOP CENTER

*Refer to **Quilt Assembly Diagram**, page 29, for placement. Press seam allowances in each **Row** toward setting triangles and **Block B's**.*

1. Sew 2 **setting triangles**, 1 **corner setting triangle**, and 1 **Block A** together to make **Row 1**. Make 2 **Row 1's**.

2. **Rows 2 – 7** are pieced diagonally with 1 **Block A** and 1 **setting triangle** at each end. **Block A's** and **Block B's** are alternated. Sew 2 *each* of **Rows 2 – 7**.

3. Alternating **Block A's** and **Block B's**, sew 1 **corner setting triangle**, 8 **Block A's**, 7 **Block B's**, and 1 **setting triangle** together to make **Row 8**. Make 2 **Row 8's**.

4. Sew **Rows** together to complete quilt top center. Press seam allowances between **Rows** in one direction. Trim outer edge of quilt top center if needed, *making sure to leave a ¹/₄" seam allowance from the points.*

ADDING THE BORDERS

1. To determine length of **side inner borders**, measure *length* of quilt top center. Trim 2 **side inner borders** to determined length. Matching centers and corners, sew **side inner borders** to quilt top.

2. To determine length of **top/bottom inner borders**, measure *width* of quilt top center (including added borders). Trim 2 **top/bottom inner borders** to determined length. Matching centers and corners, sew **top/bottom inner borders** to quilt top.

3. Using a diagonal seam, sew 2 **border strips** together end to end to make 1 **middle border**. Make 4 **middle borders**.

4. Repeat Steps 1 – 2 to measure, trim, and sew **middle** and **outer borders** to quilt top.

COMPLETING THE QUILT

1. Follow **Quilting**, page 105, to mark, layer, and quilt as desired. Our quilt is machine quilted with a continuous leaf and twig design.

2. Cut a 27" square of binding fabric. Follow **Binding**, page 108, to bind quilt using 2"w bias binding with mitered corners.

Quilt Assembly Diagram

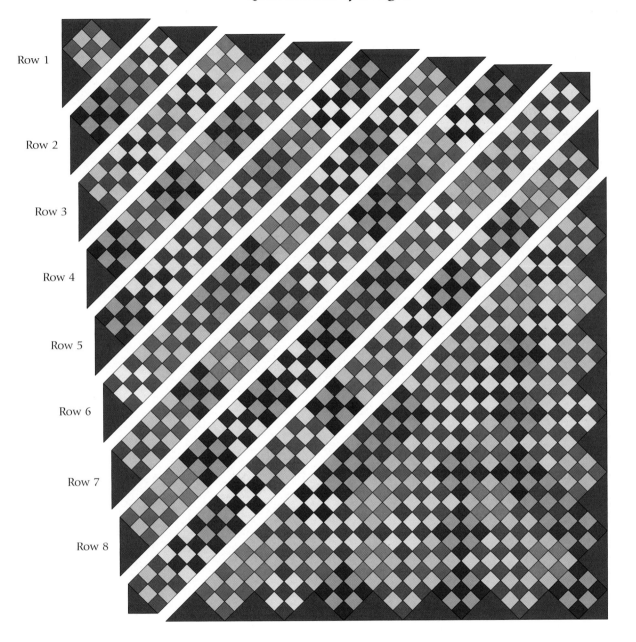

Row 1
Row 2
Row 3
Row 4
Row 5
Row 6
Row 7
Row 8

Stella Blue

Finished Quilt Size: 78$\frac{1}{2}$" x 78$\frac{1}{2}$" (199 cm x 199 cm)
Finished Block Size: 12" x 12" (30 cm x 30 cm)

Pieced by Carrie Nelson.
Quilted by Diane Tricka.

Mark (Carrie's brother) is a long-time Grateful Dead fan. Accordingly, he named his beloved Labrador retriever after one of his favorite songs. And since the large stars on this quilt are blue, and *stella* is another word for *stars*, Carrie thought calling this quilt "Stella Blue" seemed a nice way to appreciate a wonderful dog and a "pretty nice brother." And, yes, Mark already has dibs on the quilt.

YARDAGE REQUIREMENTS

Yardage is based on 43"/44" (109 cm/112 cm) wide fabric with a "usable" width of 40" (102 cm) after trimming selvages and shrinkage.

6¼ yds (5.7 m) *total of* assorted light print fabrics

3¾ yds (3.4 m) *total of* assorted blue print fabrics

1⅞ yds (1.7 m) *total of* assorted red, gold, and blue dark print fabrics

7¼ yds (6.6 m) of fabric for backing

⅞ yd (80 cm) of fabric for binding

You will also need:

87" x 87" (221 cm x 221 cm) square of batting

CUTTING OUT THE PIECES

*Follow **Rotary Cutting**, page 103, to cut fabric. All measurements include ¼" seam allowances.*

From assorted light print fabrics:

- Cut 196 **small squares** 2" x 2".
- Cut 240 **medium squares** 3½" x 3½".
- Cut 8 **large squares** 3⅞" x 3⅞".
- Cut 196 **small rectangles** 3½" x 2".
- Cut 112 **large rectangles** 6½" x 3½".

From assorted blue print fabrics:

- Cut 200 **medium squares** 3½" x 3½".
- Cut 8 **large squares** 3⅞" x 3⅞".
- Cut 88 **large rectangles** 6½" x 3½".

From assorted red, gold, and blue dark print fabrics:

For each of the 49 small stars,

- Cut 1 **medium center square** 3½" x 3½"

    or

    4 **small center squares** 2" x 2" (2 each of 2 different colors).

- Cut 8 **star point squares** 2" x 2" from 1 color that contrasts with center of star.

Note: Pin dark print pieces of each small star together or place pieces in sandwich bags or envelopes.

MAKING THE SMALL STAR UNITS

*Follow **Piecing**, page 103, and **Pressing**, page 104, to assemble the quilt top. Use ¼" seam allowances throughout. For each **Small Star Unit**, select 4 light print **small squares**, 4 light print **small rectangles**, and the red, gold, and blue dark print pieces for 1 small star.*

1. If using **small center squares** (instead of **medium center square**), sew 4 **small center squares** together to make **Unit 1**.

Unit 1

2. With right sides together, place 1 **star point square** on 1 end of 1 light print **small rectangle** and stitch diagonally. Trim ¼" from stitching line (**Fig. 1**). Open up and press seam allowances toward triangle (**Fig. 2**).

Fig. 1

Fig. 2

3. Place another **star point square** on opposite end of **small rectangle**. Stitch and trim as shown in **Fig. 3**. Open up and press seam allowances toward triangle to complete **Flying Geese Unit A**. Make 4 **Flying Geese Unit A's**.

Fig. 3

Flying Geese Unit A (make 4)

4. Sew 1 **Flying Geese Unit A** and 2 light print **small squares** together to make **Unit 2**. Press seam allowances toward **small squares**. Make 2 **Unit 2's**.

Unit 2 (make 2)

5. Sew 2 **Flying Geese Unit A's** and 1 center of **Small Star Unit** (1 **medium center square** *or* 1 **Unit 1**) together to make **Unit 3**. Press seam allowances toward center.

Unit 3

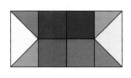

6. Sew 2 **Unit 2's** and **Unit 3** together to make **Small Star Unit**. Press seam allowances toward **Unit 3**.

Small Star Unit

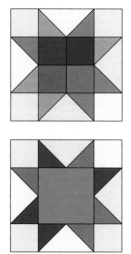

7. Repeat Steps 1 – 6 to make 49 **Small Star Units**.

MAKING THE BLOCKS

1. Using blue print **medium squares** and light print **large rectangles**, follow Steps 2 – 3 of **Making the Small Star Units**, page 32, to make 100 **Flying Geese Unit B's**.

Flying Geese Unit B (make 100)

2. Sew 1 **Flying Geese Unit B** and 2 light print **medium squares** together to make **Unit 4**. Press seam allowances toward **medium squares**. Make 32 **Unit 4's**.

Unit 4 (make 32)

3. Sew 2 **Flying Geese Unit B's** and 1 **Small Star Unit** together to make **Unit 5**. Press seam allowances toward **Small Star Unit**. Make 16 **Unit 5's**.

Unit 5 (make 16)

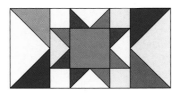

4. Sew 2 **Unit 4's** and 1 **Unit 5** together to make **Block**. Press seam allowances toward **Unit 4's**. Make 16 **Blocks**.

Block (make 16)

5. Sew 2 **Flying Geese Unit B's** and 1 **Small Star Unit** together to make **Inner Partial Block**. Press seam allowances toward **Small Star Unit**. Make 12 **Inner Partial Blocks**.

Inner Partial Block (make 12)

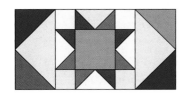

6. Sew 1 light print **large rectangle**, 1 **Small Star Unit**, and 1 **Flying Geese Unit B** together to make **Outer Partial Block**. Press seam allowances toward **large rectangle** and **Flying Geese Unit B**. Make 12 **Outer Partial Blocks**.

Outer Partial Block (make 12)

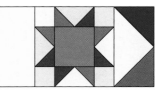

ASSEMBLING THE QUILT TOP CENTER

*Refer to **Quilt Assembly Diagram**, page 37, for placement and orientation.*

1. Sew 4 **Blocks** and 3 **Outer Partial Blocks** together to make **Row 1**. Press seam allowances toward **Blocks**. Make 2 **Row 1's**.
2. Sew 2 **Outer Partial Blocks**, 3 **Small Star Units**, and 2 **Inner Partial Blocks** together to make **Row 2**. Press seam allowances toward **Small Star Units** and **Inner Partial Blocks**. Make 3 **Row 2's**.
3. Sew 4 **Blocks** and 3 **Inner Partial Blocks** together to make **Row 3**. Press seam allowances toward **Blocks**. Make 2 **Row 3's**.
4. Sew **Rows** together to make quilt top center. Press seam allowances toward **Row 2's**.

ADDING THE BORDERS

1. Using light print **medium squares** and blue print **large rectangles**, follow Steps 2 – 3 of **Making the Small Star Units**, page 32, to make 88 **Flying Geese Unit C's**. Press seam allowances toward **large rectangles**.

Flying Geese Unit C (make 88)

A Note from Carrie

About Pieced Borders:

When it comes to pieced borders, sometimes you get it right the first time. Most of the time, we need to "adjust." In this case, it means "adjusting" the length of the pieced border. The easiest and least noticeable way to make the border strip the same length as the quilt top is to make some of the seams just a skosh bigger or smaller. If you need to shorten the border strip, sew a line of stitching just inside the first seam line. If you need a longer borders strip, sew a line of stitching just outside the first seam line and then remove the first line of stitching. That $^1/_{16}$" difference in seam will add up to $^1/_8$" between the two fabrics. An eighth of an inch removed eight times quickly adds up to an inch. Just make sure that you randomly space the larger/smaller seams so that they aren't obvious.

2. Sew 22 **Flying Geese Unit C's** together to make 1 **border**. Press seam allowances toward points of **Flying Geese Units** or press open. Make 4 **borders**. *(Note that 5 of the flying geese are turned differently in the left side border.)*

3. Draw diagonal line (corner to corner) on wrong side of each light print **large square**. With right sides together, place 1 light print **large square** on top of 1 blue print **large square**. Stitch seam $^1/_4$" from each side of drawn line (**Fig. 4**).

Fig. 4

4. Cut along drawn line and press seam allowances toward darker fabric to make 2 **Triangle-Squares**. Make 16 **Triangle-Squares**.

Triangle-Squares (make 16)

5. Sew 4 **Triangle-Squares** together to make **Corner Border Unit**. Make 4 **Corner Border Units**.

Corner Border Unit (make 4)

6. Sew 1 **Corner Border Unit** to *each* end of **top** and **bottom borders**.

7. Matching centers and corners and easing any fullness, sew **side**, **top**, and then **bottom borders** to quilt top. Press seam allowances toward center section of quilt top.

COMPLETING THE QUILT

. Follow **Quilting**, page 105, to mark, layer, and quilt as desired. (*Note: Stay-stitching around the quilt top approximately 1/8" from the edge before quilting will help stabilize the edge and prevent any seams from separating.*) Our quilt is machine quilted with a combination of straight and curved lines.

2. Cut a 28" square of binding fabric. Follow **Binding**, page 108, to bind quilt using 2"w bias binding with mitered corners.

Quilt Assembly Diagram

Uptown Girl

Finished Quilt Size: 68¹/₂" x 79¹/₂" (174 cm x 202 cm)
Finished Block Size: 10" x 10" (25 cm x 25 cm)

Pieced by Carrie Nelson
Quilted by Sharon Brooks

This quilt isn't named after the Billy Joel tune, although Carrie thinks it's a great song. She came to the title because she's no longer down on the farm, but living "up in town." These Farmer's Daughter blocks have a new twist … in place of the traditional Nine-Patch centers are Churn Dashes, Shoo-Flies, Ohio Stars, and even Four-Patch Nine-Patches.

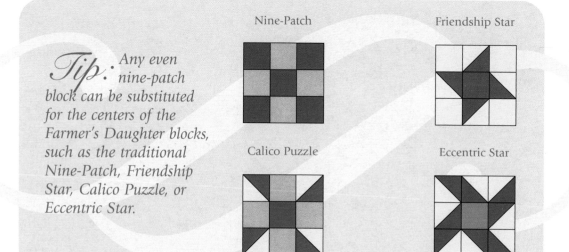

Tip: Any even nine-patch block can be substituted for the centers of the Farmer's Daughter blocks, such as the traditional Nine-Patch, Friendship Star, Calico Puzzle, or Eccentric Star.

Nine-Patch

Friendship Star

Calico Puzzle

Eccentric Star

YARDAGE REQUIREMENTS

*Yardage is based on 43"/44" (109 cm/112 cm) wide fabric with a "usable" width of 40" (102 cm) after trimming selvages and shrinkage. Yardage requirements may vary depending on color and **Block Center** variations.*

$3^3/_8$ yds (3.1 m) *total* of assorted light/medium print fabrics

5 yds (4.6 m) *total* of assorted medium/dark print fabrics

1 yd (91 cm) of rust print for sashings

$^3/_4$ yd (69 cm) of gold print for inner border and sashing squares

$2^1/_4$ yds (2.1 m) of black print fabric for outer border

5 yds (4.6 m) of fabric for backing

$^7/_8$ yd (80 cm) of fabric for binding

You will also need:

77" x 88" (196 cm x 224 cm) rectangle of batting

Tip: Mix up the color value of the block center backgrounds by using medium and dark fabrics instead of the more traditional light background. The same goes for the contrast of values in each block center. Using a high-contrast combination for some block centers and a low-contrast combination for other block centers will make the same design look very different from block to block.

41

CUTTING OUT THE PIECES

*Follow **Rotary Cutting**, page 103, to cut fabric. All strips are cut across the width of the fabric unless otherwise noted. Borders include an extra 4" of length for "insurance" and will be trimmed after assembling quilt top center. All other measurements include ¹/₄" seam allowances. Each "set" should be cut from one fabric or similar color fabrics.*

You will need to cut centers for 30 blocks. Our quilt has 11 Ohio Star, 6 Shoo-Fly, 7 Four-Patch Nine-Patch, and 6 Churn Dash **Block Centers**. You may use any combination.

For *each* Ohio Star:
- Cut 4 **small squares** 2¹/₂" x 2¹/₂" and 1 **large square** 3¹/₄" x 3¹/₄" from one print.
- Cut 2 **large squares** 3¹/₄" x 3¹/₄" from a second print.
- Cut 1 **large square** 3¹/₄" x 3¹/₄" from a third print.
- Cut 1 **center square** 2¹/₂" x 2¹/₂" from a fourth print.

For *each* Shoo-Fly:
- Cut 4 **small squares** 2¹/₂" x 2¹/₂" and 2 **large squares** 2⁷/₈" x 2⁷/₈" from one print.
- Cut 2 **large squares** 2⁷/₈" x 2⁷/₈" and 1 **center square** 2¹/₂" x 2¹/₂" from a second print.

For *each* Churn Dash:
- Cut 2 **large squares** 2⁷/₈" x 2⁷/₈", 1 **center square** 2¹/₂" x 2¹/₂", and 4 **rectangles** 2¹/₂" x 1¹/₂" from one print.
- Cut 2 **large squares** 2⁷/₈" x 2⁷/₈" and 4 **rectangles** 2¹/₂" x 1¹/₂" from a second print.

For *each* Four-Patch Nine-Patch:
- Cut 4 **large squares** 2¹/₂" x 2¹/₂" from one print.
- Cut 20 **small squares** 1¹/₂" x 1¹/₂" from assorted prints.

From assorted light/medium print fabrics:
- Cut 30 sets of 4 **squares** 2¹/₂" x 2¹/₂" and 4 **rectangles** 2¹/₂" x 6¹/₂".

From assorted medium/dark print fabrics:
- Cut 30 sets of 8 **squares** 2¹/₂" x 2¹/₂".
- Cut 12 **large border squares** 2¹/₂" x 2¹/₂".
- Cut 32 **small border squares** 1¹/₂" x 1¹/₂". *(Some may be cut from light/medium print fabrics if desired.)*

From rust print fabric:
- Cut 3 strips 10¹/₂"w. From these strips, cut 71 **sashing strips** 10¹/₂" x 1¹/₂".

From gold print fabric:
- Cut 7 **border strips** 2¹/₂"w.
- Cut 2 strips 1¹/₂"w. From these strips, cut 42 **sashing squares** 1¹/₂" x 1¹/₂".

From black print fabric:
- Cut 2 *lengthwise* **side outer borders** 4¹/₂" x 75¹/₂".
- Cut 2 *lengthwise* **top/bottom outer borders** 4¹/₂" x 64¹/₂".

MAKING THE BLOCK CENTERS

*Follow **Piecing**, page 103, and **Pressing**, page 104. Use ¹/₄" seam allowances throughout. Make a total of 30 **Block Centers**. Arrows on diagrams indicate direction to press seam allowances.*

Ohio Star

1. Draw diagonal line (corner to corner) on wrong side of 2 **large squares** of same print.
2. With right sides together, place 1 marked **large square** on top of 1 unmarked **large square**. Stitch seam ¹/₄" from each side of drawn line (**Fig. 1**).

Fig. 1

3. Cut along drawn line and press seam allowances toward darker fabric to make 2 **Triangle-Square A's**.

Triangle-Square A's (make 2)

4. Repeat Steps 2 – 3 using remaining **large squares** to make 2 **Triangle-Square B's**.

Triangle-Square B's (make 2)

On wrong side of **Triangle-Square A's**, draw diagonal line (corner to corner and perpendicular to seam). With contrasting fabrics facing and right sides together, place 1 **Triangle-Square A** on top of 1 **Triangle-Square B**. Stitch seam ¹/₄" from each side of drawn line (**Fig. 2**). Cut apart along drawn line to make 2 **Hourglass Units**; press **Hourglass Units** open. Make 4 **Hourglass Units**.

Fig. 2

Hourglass Unit (make 4)

Sew 2 **small squares** and 1 **Hourglass Unit** together to make **Unit 1**. Make 2 **Unit 1's**.

Unit 1 (make 2)

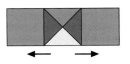

Sew 2 **Hourglass Units** and **center square** together to make **Unit 2**.

Unit 2

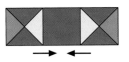

9. Sew 2 **Unit 1's** and **Unit 2** together to make **Ohio Star**.

Ohio Star

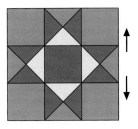

Shoo-Fly

1. Draw diagonal line (corner to corner) on wrong side of 2 **large squares** of same print.
2. With right sides together, place 1 marked **large square** on top of 1 unmarked **large square**. Stitch seam ¹/₄" from each side of drawn line (**Fig. 3**).

Fig. 3

3. Cut along drawn line and press open to make 2 **Triangle-Square C's**. Make 4 **Triangle-Square C's**.

Triangle-Square C (make 4)

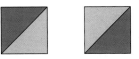

4. Sew 2 **Triangle Square C's** and 1 **small square** together to make **Unit 3**. Make 2 **Unit 3's**.

Unit 3 (make 2)

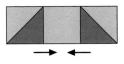

5. Sew 2 **small squares** and **center square** together to make **Unit 4**.

Unit 4

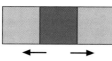

6. Sew 2 **Unit 3's** and **Unit 4** together to make **Shoo-Fly**.

Shoo-Fly

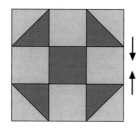

Churn Dash

1. Draw diagonal line (corner to corner) on wrong side of 2 **large squares** of same print.

2. With right sides together, place 1 marked **large square** on top of 1 unmarked **large square**. Stitch seam $\frac{1}{4}$" from each side of drawn line (**Fig. 4**).

Fig. 4

3. Cut along drawn line and press seam allowances toward darker fabric make 2 **Triangle-Square D's**. Make 4 **Triangle-Square D's**.

Triangle-Square D's (make 4)

4. Sew 2 **rectangles** of different prints together to mak Unit 5. Make 4 **Unit 5's**.

Unit 5 (make 4)

5. Sew 2 **Triangle Square D's** and 1 **Unit 5** together to make **Unit 6**. Make 2 **Unit 6's**.

Unit 6 (make 2)

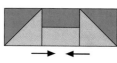

6. Sew 2 **Unit 5's** and **center square** together to make **Unit 7**.

Unit 7

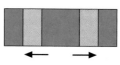

7. Sew 2 **Unit 6's** and **Unit 7** together to make **Churn Dash**.

Churn Dash

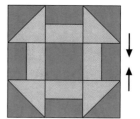

our-Patch Nine-Patch

Sew 4 **small squares** together to make **Unit 8**. Make 5 **Unit 8's**.

Unit 8 (make 5)

Sew 2 **Unit 8's** and 1 **large square** together to make **Unit 9**. Make 2 **Unit 9's**.

Unit 9 (make 2)

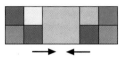

Sew 2 **large squares** and 1 **Unit 8** together to make **Unit 10**.

Unit 10

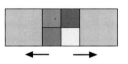

Sew 2 **Unit 9's** and **Unit 10** together to make **Four-Patch Nine-Patch**.

Four-Patch Nine-Patch

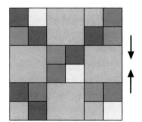

MAKING THE BLOCKS

1. Select 1 **Block Center**, 1 set of light/medium **squares** and **rectangles**, and 1 set of medium/dark **squares**.
2. With right sides together, place 1 medium/dark **square** on 1 end of 1 light/medium **rectangle** and stitch diagonally. Trim $^1/_4$" from stitching line (**Fig. 5**). Open up and press seam allowances toward triangle (**Fig. 6**).

Fig. 5

Fig. 6

3. Place another medium/dark **square** on opposite end of light/medium **rectangle**. Stitch and trim as shown in **Fig. 7**. Open up and press seam allowances toward triangle to complete **Unit 11**. Make 4 **Unit 11's**.

Fig. 7

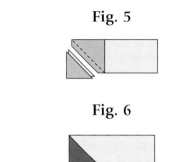

Unit 11 (make 4)

4. Sew 2 light/medium **squares** and 1 **Unit 11** together to make **Unit 12**. Press seam allowances toward **squares**. Make 2 **Unit 12's**.

Unit 12 (make 2)

5. Sew 2 **Unit 11's** and 1 **Block Center** together to make **Unit 13**. Press seam allowances open or toward **Block Center**.

Unit 13

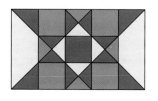

6. Sew 2 **Unit 12's** and **Unit 13** together to make **Block**. Press seam allowances open or toward **Unit 13**. Make a total of 30 **Blocks**.

Blocks (make a *total* of 30)

ASSEMBLING THE QUILT TOP CENTER

*Refer to **Quilt Top Diagram**, page 47, for placement.*

1. Sew 5 **Blocks** and 6 **sashing strips** together to ma[...] Row. Make 6 **Rows**.
2. Sew 6 **sashing squares** and 5 **sashing strips** together to make **Sashing Row**. Make 7 **Sashing Rows**.
3. Sew **Sashing Rows** and **Rows** together to complete[...] quilt top center.

ADDING THE BORDERS

1. Using diagonal seams, sew **border strips** togeth[...] end to end (**Fig. 8**) to make 1 continuous **inner** **border strip**.

Fig. 8

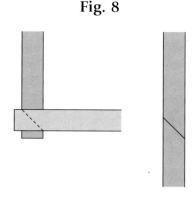

2. To determine length of **side inner borders**, measu[...] *length* of quilt top center. Cut 2 **side inner borders** from **inner border strip** to determined length. Do *not* sew to quilt top center at this time.
3. To determine length of **top/bottom inner borders**, measure *width* of quilt top center. Cut 2 **top/botto[...]** **inner borders** from **inner border strip** to determined length. Do *not* sew to quilt top center [...] this time.

Four-Patch Nine-Patch

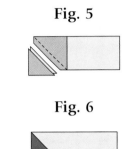

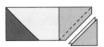

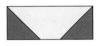

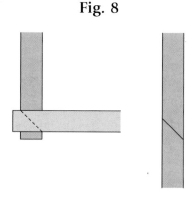

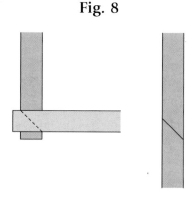

- Sew 1 **large border square** to each end of **top/bottom inner borders**.
- Matching centers and corners, sew **side**, **top**, and then **bottom inner borders** to quilt top.
- Sew 4 **small border squares** together to make **Unit 14**. Make 8 **Unit 14's**.

Unit 14 (make 8)

- Sew 2 **large border squares** and 2 **Unit 14's** together to make **Corner Border Unit**. Make 4 **Corner Border Units**.

Corner Border Unit (make 4)

- Repeat Steps 2 – 3 to measure and trim **outer borders**.
- Sew 1 **Corner Border Unit** to each end of **top/bottom outer borders**, making sure **Corner Border Units** are rotated correctly.
0. Matching centers and corners, sew **side**, **top**, and then **bottom outer borders** to quilt top.

COMPLETING THE QUILT

1. Follow **Quilting**, page 105, to mark, layer, and quilt as desired. Our quilt is machine quilted with an all-over pumpkin vine pattern.
2. Cut a 27" square of binding fabric. Follow **Binding**, page 108, to bind quilt using 2"w bias binding with mitered corners.

Quilt Top Diagram

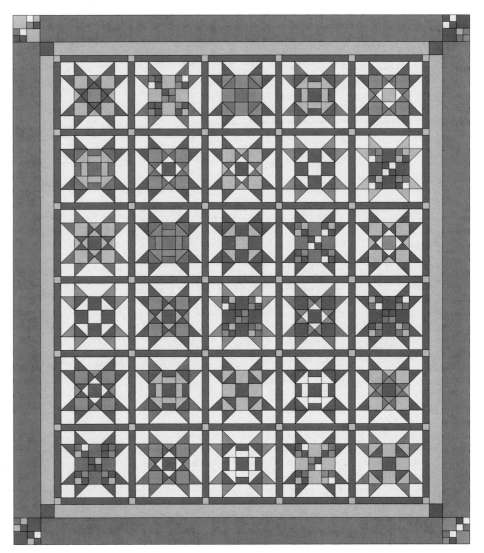

Radio Flyer

Finished Quilt Size: 71$\frac{1}{2}$" x 83$\frac{1}{2}$" (182 cm x 212 cm)
Finished Block Size: 6" x 6" (15 cm x 15 cm)

Pieced by Carrie Nelson.
Quilted by Darlene Johannis.

This quilt was "born" when Carrie saw a picture of an antique scrap quilt, identified only as … "scrap quilt." She was unable to find the block in any of her block encyclopedias or block books, but thought it looked a little like a Turkey Giblets Block, only without the curves.

Whatever the proper name of the original quilt design, Carrie updated her version to avoid the "dreaded T-word" (templates). By changing the angle of some of the pieces, she found that she could get a very similar design by a much simpler method.

YARDAGE REQUIREMENTS

Yardage is based on 43"/44" (109 cm/112 cm) wide fabric with a "usable" width of 40" (102 cm) after trimming selvages and shrinkage.

- $4^1/_8$ yds (3.8 m) *total* of assorted dark print fabrics
- $4^1/_8$ yds (3.8 m) *total* of assorted light print fabrics
- $^5/_8$ yd (57 cm) of tan stripe for inner border
- $2^5/_8$ yds (2.4 m) of red print for outer border
- *6$^3/_4$ yds (6.2 m) of fabric for backing
- $^7/_8$ yd (80 cm) of fabric for binding

You will also need:

- 80" x 92" (203 cm x 234 cm) rectangle of batting
- *Yardage is based on 3 lengths of fabric, which allows for a larger backing for long arm quilting. If you are using another quilting method, 2 lengths, or $5^1/_8$ yds (4.7 m), will be adequate.

CUTTING OUT THE PIECES

*Follow **Rotary Cutting**, page 103, to cut fabric. All strips are cut across the width of the fabric unless otherwise noted. Borders include an extra 4" of length for "insurance" and will be trimmed after assembling quilt top center. All other measurements include $^1/_4$" seam allowances.*

From assorted dark print fabrics:
- Cut 60 **large squares** $6^7/_8$" x $6^7/_8$".
- Cut 120 **medium squares** 3" x 3".
- Cut 120 **small squares** $2^5/_8$" x $2^5/_8$".

From assorted light print fabrics:
- Cut 60 **large squares** $6^7/_8$" x $6^7/_8$".
- Cut 120 **medium squares** 3" x 3".
- Cut 120 **small squares** $2^5/_8$" x $2^5/_8$".

From tan stripe fabric:
- Cut 9 **border strips** 2"w.

From red print fabric:
- Cut 2 *lengthwise* **side outer borders** $4^1/_2$" x $87^1/_2$".
- Cut 2 *lengthwise* **top/bottom outer borders** $4^1/_2$" x $75^1/_2$".

MAKING THE BLOCKS

*Follow **Piecing**, page 103, and **Pressing**, page 104, to assemble the quilt top. Use $^1/_4$" seam allowances throughout.*

1. With right sides together, place 1 light print **medium square** on 1 corner of 1 dark print **large square** and stitch diagonally. Trim $^1/_4$" from stitching line (**Fig. 1**). Open up and press seam allowances toward triangle (**Fig. 2**).

Fig. 1   **Fig. 2**

2. Add another light print **medium square** to opposite corner of dark print **large square** as shown in **Fig. 3**. Open up and press seam allowances toward triangle (**Fig. 4**).

Fig. 3   **Fig. 4**

3. Add 1 light print **small square** to each remaining corner of **large square** as shown in **Fig. 5**, pressing seam allowances toward triangles, to make **Unit 1**. Make 60 **Unit 1's**.

Fig. 5   **Unit 1** (make 60)

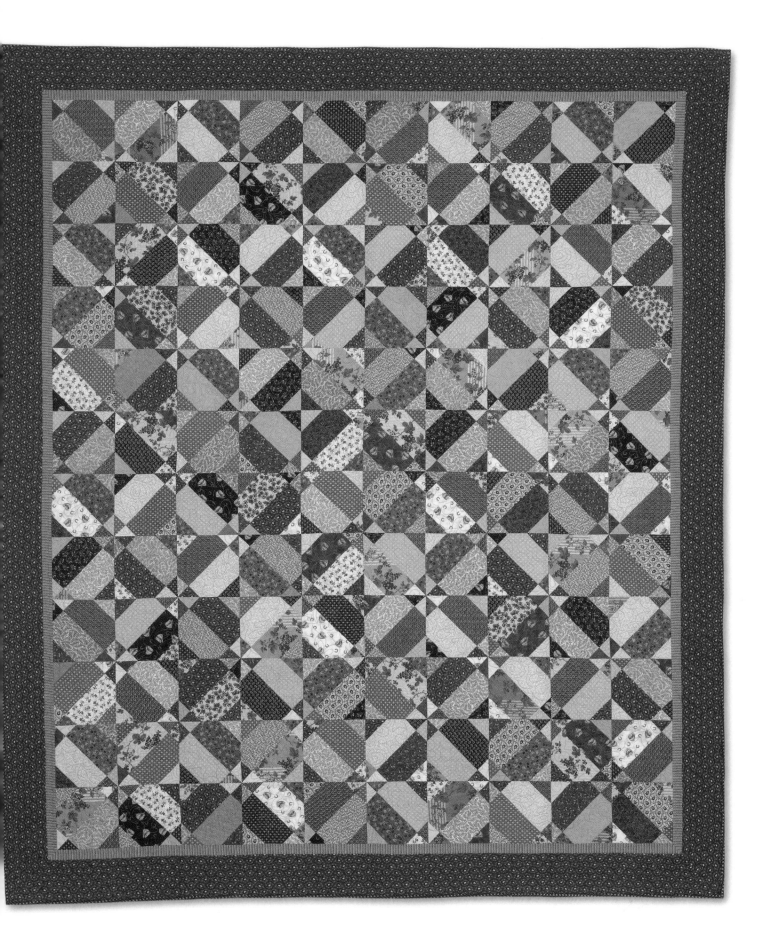

51

4. Repeat Steps 1 – 3, page 50, using light print **large squares** and dark print **medium** and **small squares**, pressing seam allowances toward **large square**, to make 60 **Unit 2's**.

Unit 2 (make 60)

5. Draw diagonal line (corner to corner) on wrong side of each **Unit 2** with line going through large triangles. With right sides together and matching large triangles, place 1 **Unit 2** on top of 1 **Unit 1**. Stitch seam ¹⁄₄" from each side of drawn line (**Fig. 6**).

Fig. 6

6. Cut along drawn line and press open, pressing seam allowances toward dark center, to make 2 **Blocks**. Make 120 **Blocks**.

Blocks (make 120)

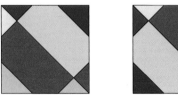

ASSEMBLING THE QUILT TOP CENTER

When pressing the seam allowances between blocks and between rows, Carrie found that pressing them open worked best. Pressing seam allowances open will keep the points sharp and reduce the amount of bulk in the seams.

Tip: *When sewing the Blocks and Rows together, pay close attention to where the snowball corners of adjacent Blocks meet. If necessary, pin the points so that they match perfectly, and then ease any excess. This is most easily done by putting the side with the excess on the bottom when the seam is being stitched to let the feed dog of your sewing machine do the easing for you.*

1. Referring to photo, page 51, and **Quilt Top Diagram**, page 53, for placement and **Block** orientation, arrange **Blocks** on floor or design wall in a manner pleasing to you. *Note: When the **Blocks** are positioned correctly, the squares at the intersections of each **Block** should alternate between a pinwheel and a quarter-triangle square.*
2. Sew 10 **Blocks** together, making sure **Blocks** are turned correctly, to make **Row**. Make 12 **Rows**.
3. Sew **Rows** together to make center section of quilt top.

ADDING THE BORDERS

1. Using diagonal seams, sew **border strips** together end to end to make 1 continuous **inner border strip** (**Fig. 7**).

Fig. 7

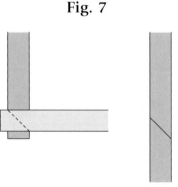

2. Cut 2 **side inner borders** to 87¹⁄₂"l and 2 **top/bottom inner borders** to 75¹⁄₂"l.
3. Sew 1 **side inner border** and 1 **side outer border** together lengthwise to make 1 **side border**. Make 2 **side borders**.

Sew **top inner border** and **top outer border** together lengthwise to make **top border**. Repeat to make **bottom border**.

Mark the center of each edge of quilt top. Mark the center of inner edge of each **border**. Measure across center of quilt top. Beginning at center of **top border**, measure ¹/₂ the width of the quilt top in both directions and mark. Matching raw edges and marks on **top border** with center and corners of quilt top and easing in any fullness, pin **top border** to quilt top. Sew **top border** to quilt top, beginning and ending exactly ¹/₄" from each corner of quilt top. Backstitch at beginning and ending of stitching to reinforce. Repeat Steps 5 – 6 to sew **bottom** and then **side borders** to quilt top. Fold 1 corner of quilt top diagonally with right sides together and matching edges. Aligning ruler with fold, use ruler to mark stitching line as shown in **Fig. 8**. Sew on drawn line, backstitching at beginning and ending of stitching. Turn mitered corner right side up. Check to make sure corner will lie flat with no gaps or puckers. Trim seam allowances to ¹/₄" and press to one side. Repeat for other corners.

Fig. 8

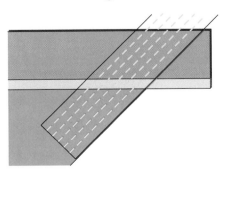

COMPLETING THE QUILT

1. Follow **Quilting**, page 105, to mark, layer, and quilt as desired. Our quilt is free-motion machine quilted with a swirl pattern.
2. Cut a 27" square of binding fabric. Follow **Binding**, page 108, to bind quilt using 2"w bias binding with mitered corners.

Quilt Top Diagram

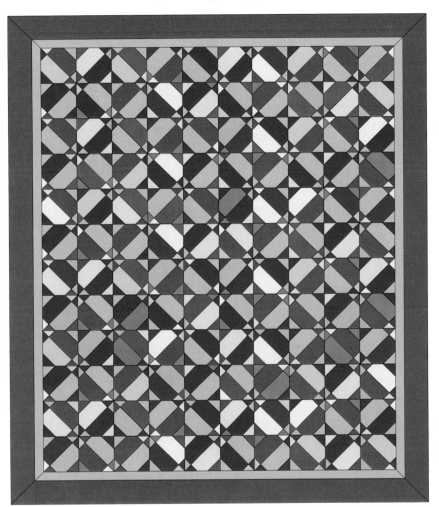

Wild Irish Rose

Finished Quilt Size: 85$\frac{1}{4}$" x 97$\frac{1}{2}$" (217 cm x 248 cm)
Finished Block Size: 8$\frac{3}{4}$" x 8$\frac{3}{4}$" (22 cm x 22 cm)

Pieced by Judy Adams.
Quilted by Sharon Brooks.

Carrie loves Irish Chain quilts and went "wild" with this nontraditional, very scrappy version. The blocks are made the same, but turned on point to bring a brand new look to this old favorite.

While the lovely rose prints make this quilt charming, Carrie sees bright chains with a black-and-white background in her future.

YARDAGE REQUIREMENTS

Yardage is based on 43"/44" (109 cm/112 cm) wide fabric with a "usable" width of 40" (102 cm) after trimming selvages and shrinkage.

6⅞ yds (6.3 m) *total* of assorted print fabrics for chains and outer border

3⅝ yds (3.3 m) of cream and white print fabric

1⅝ yds (1.5 m) of cream floral fabric

7⅞ yds (7.2 m) of fabric for backing

1 yd (91 cm) of fabric for binding

You will also need:

94" x 106" (239 cm x 269 cm) rectangle of batting

CUTTING OUT THE PIECES

Follow Rotary Cutting, page 103, to cut fabric. All strips are cut across the width of the fabric unless otherwise noted. All measurements include ¼" seam allowances.

From assorted print fabric:
- Cut 187 **medium strips** 2¼" x 20".
- Cut 16 **small strips** 1½" x 8".
- Cut 22 **squares** 2¼" x 2¼".

From cream and white print fabric:
- Cut 8 **large strips** 5¾" x 20".
- Cut 43 **medium strips** 2¼" x 20".
- Cut 9 **border strips** 1¾"w.
- Cut 13 strips 2¼"w. From these strips, cut 4 **large rectangles** 2¼" x 11" and 44 **small rectangles** 2¼" x 9".

From cream floral fabric:
- Cut 10 **large strips** 5¾" x 20".
- Cut 2 strips 8¾"w. From these strips, cut 6 squares 8¾" x 8¾". Cut squares *twice* diagonally to make 24 **large triangles**. (You will use 22 and have 2 left over.)
- Cut 2 squares 4⅝" x 4⅝". Cut squares *once* diagonally to make 4 **small triangles**.

MAKING THE BLOCKS AND SETTING TRIANGLES

Follow Piecing, page 103, and Pressing, page 104, to make quilt top. Use ¼" seam allowances throughout.

1. Sew 4 assorted print **medium strips** and 1 cream and white **medium strip** together with cream and white **medium strip** in the center to make **Strip Set A**. Press seam allowances toward 2nd and 4th **medium strips**. Make 11 **Strip Set A's**. Cut across **Strip Set A's** at 2¼" intervals to make 84 **Unit 1's**.

Strip Set A
(make 11)

Unit 1
(make 84)

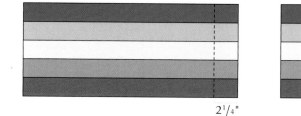

2. Sew 5 assorted print **medium strips** together to make **Strip Set B**. Press seam allowances toward 1st, 3rd, and 5th **medium strips**. Make 11 **Strip Set B's**. Cut across **Strip Set B's** at 2¼" intervals to make 84 **Unit 2's**.

Strip Set B
(make 11)

Unit 2
(make 84)

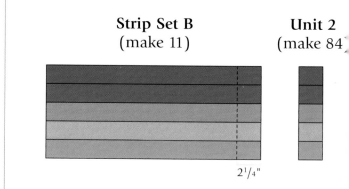

3. Sew 2 cream and white **medium strips** and 3 assorted print **medium strips** together with cream and white **medium strips** on the top and bottom to make **Strip Set C**. Press seam allowances toward 2nd and 4th **medium strips**. Make 6 **Strip Set C's**. Cut across **Strip Set C's** at 2¹/₄" intervals to make 42 **Unit 3's**.

Strip Set C (make 6) **Unit 3** (make 42)

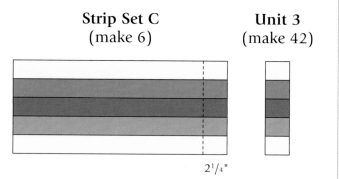

2¹/₄"

4. Sew 2 **Unit 1's**, 2 **Unit 2's**, and 1 **Unit 3** together to make **Irish Chain Block**. Press seam allowances toward **Unit 1's** and **Unit 3**. Make 42 **Irish Chain Blocks**.

Irish Chain Block (make 42)

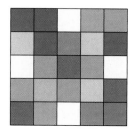

5. Sew 2 assorted print **medium strips** and 1 cream and white **large strip** together to make **Strip Set D**. Make 8 **Strip Set D's**. Press seam allowances toward **medium strips**. Cut across **Strip Set D's** at 2¹/₄" intervals to make 60 **Unit 4's**.

Strip Set D (make 8) **Unit 4** (make 60)

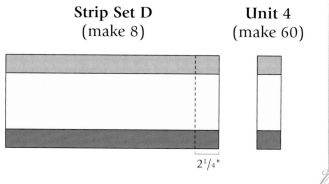

2¹/₄"

6. Sew 2 cream and white **medium strips** and 1 cream floral **large strip** together to make **Strip Set E**. Press seam allowances toward **large strip**. Make 10 **Strip Set E's**. Cut across **Strip Set E's** at 5³/₄" intervals to make 30 **Unit 5's**.

Strip Set E (make 10) **Unit 5** (make 30)

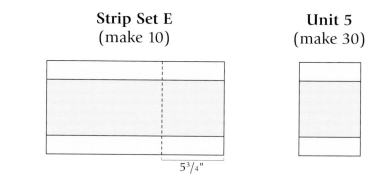

5³/₄"

7. Sew 2 **Unit 4's** and 1 **Unit 5** together to make **Alternate Block**. Press seam allowances toward **Unit 4's**. Make 30 **Alternate Blocks**.

Alternate Block (make 30)

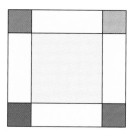

8. Sew 1 **small rectangle** and 1 **square** together to make **Unit 6**. Press seam allowances toward **square**. Make 22 **Unit 6's**.

Unit 6 (make 22)

Sew 1 **small rectangle** and 1 **large triangle** together to make **Unit 7**. Press seam allowances toward **large triangle**. Make 22 **Unit 7's**.

Unit 7 (make 22)

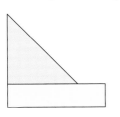

0. Sew 1 **Unit 6** and 1 **Unit 7** together; press seam allowances toward **Unit 6**. Trim rectangles as shown in **Fig. 1** to make **pieced setting triangle**. Make 22 **pieced setting triangles**.

Fig. 1

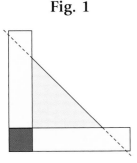

Pieced Setting Triangle (make 22)

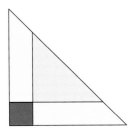

11. Sew 1 **large rectangle** and 1 **small triangle** together; press seam allowances toward **small triangle**. Trim rectangle as shown in **Fig. 2** to make **corner pieced setting triangle**. Make 4 **corner pieced setting triangles**.

Fig. 2

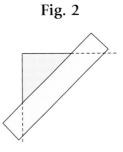

Corner Pieced Setting Triangle
(make 4)

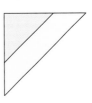

ASSEMBLING THE QUILT TOP CENTER
*Refer to **Quilt Assembly Diagram**, page 61, for placement.*

1. Sew 1 **corner pieced setting triangle**, 2 **pieced setting triangles**, and 1 **Irish Chain Block** together to make **Row 1**. Press seam allowances toward **Irish Chain Block**. Make 2 **Row 1's**.

2. **Rows 2 – 5** are pieced diagonally, with 1 **Irish Chain Block** and 1 **pieced setting triangle** at each end. **Irish Chain Blocks** and **Alternate Blocks** are alternated. Press seam allowances toward **Irish Chain Blocks**. Sew 2 *each* of **Rows 2 – 5**.

3. Sew 1 **corner pieced setting triangle**, 6 **Irish Chain Blocks**, 5 **Alternate Blocks**, and 1 **pieced setting triangle** together to make **Row 6**. Press seam allowances toward **Irish Chain Blocks**. Make 2 **Row 6's**.

4. Sew **Rows** together, pressing seam allowances in one direction, to complete quilt top center.

ADDING THE BORDERS

1. Using diagonal seams, sew **border strips** together end to end to make 1 continuous **inner border strip** (Fig. 3).

Fig. 3

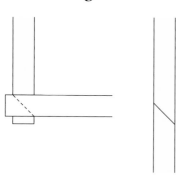

2. To determine length of **side inner borders**, measure *length* of quilt top center. Cut 2 **side inner borders** from **inner border strip** to determined length. Matching centers and corners, sew **side inner borders** to quilt top center. Press seam allowances toward **side inner borders**.

3. To determine length of **top/bottom inner borders**, measure *width* of quilt top center (including added borders). Cut 2 **top/bottom inner borders** from **inner border strip** to determined length. Matching centers and corners, sew **inner top/bottom borders** to quilt top center. Press seam allowances toward **top/bottom inner borders**.

4. Sew 4 **small strips** together to make **Strip Set F**. Press seam allowances in one direction. Make 4 **Strip Set F's**. Cut across **Strip Set F's** at $1^1/2$" intervals to make 16 **Unit 8's**.

Strip Set F (make 4) **Unit 8** (make 16)

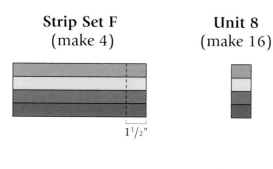

$1^1/2$"

5. Sew 4 **Unit 8's** together to make **Corner Border Unit**. Press seam allowances in one direction. Make 4 **Corner Border Units**.

Corner Border Unit (make 4)

6. Sew 6 assorted print **medium strips** together to make **Strip Set G**. Press seam allowances in one direction. Make 9 **Strip Set G's**. Cut across **Strip Set G's** at $4^1/2$" intervals to make 34 **Border Units**.

Strip Set G (make 9) **Border Unit** (make 34)

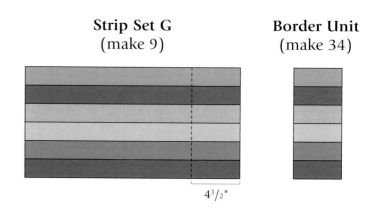

$4^1/2$"

7. Sew 9 **Border Units** together end to end to make **side outer border**. Make 2 **side outer borders**.

8. Sew 8 **Border Units** together end to end to make **top outer border**. Repeat to make **bottom outer border**.

9. To determine length of **side outer borders**, measure *length* of quilt top center. Remove rectangles and/or make a few seams between rectangles larger or smaller to make length of **side borders** equal to determined length. Do not sew **borders** to quilt top center at this time.

10. To determine length of **top/bottom borders**, measure *width* of quilt top center. Remove rectangles and/or make a few seams between rectangles larger or smaller to make length of **top/bottom borders** equal to determined length. Do not sew **borders** to quilt top center at this time.

11. Sew 1 **Corner Border Unit** to *each* end of **top** and **bottom borders**. Press seam allowances away from **Corner Border Units**.

12. Matching centers and corners, sew **side**, **top**, and then **bottom outer borders** to quilt top. Press seam allowances toward **inner borders**.

COMPLETING THE QUILT

. Follow **Quilting**, page 105, to mark, layer, and quilt as desired. *(Note: Stay-stitching around the quilt top approximately ¹/8" from the edge before quilting will help stabilize the edge and prevent any seams from separating.)* Our quilt is machine quilted. A repeating leaf and loop pattern is quilted through the chain portion, a leaf pattern is quilted in the cream and white areas and outer borders, and a flower pattern is quilted in each cream floral square and triangle.

2. Cut a 30" square of binding fabric. Follow **Binding**, page 108, to bind quilt using 2"w bias binding with mitered corners.

Quilt Assembly Diagram

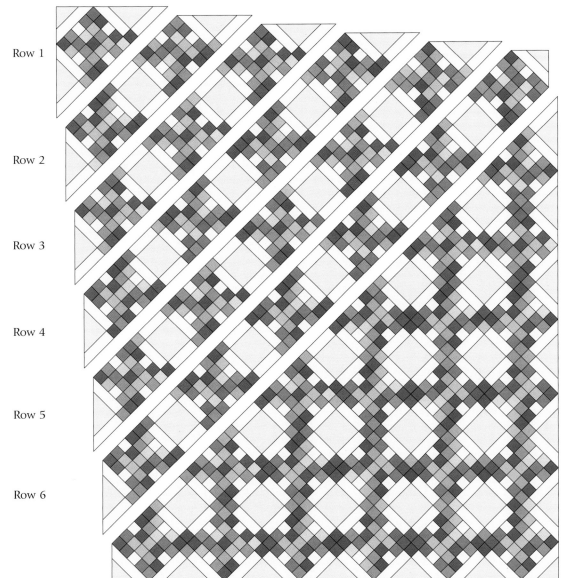

Row 1

Row 2

Row 3

Row 4

Row 5

Row 6

Rosie's Posies

Finished Quilt Size: 75 1/2" x 83" (192 cm x 211 cm)
Finished Block Size: 7 1/2" x 7 1/2" (19 cm x 19 cm)

Pieced by Sue Maitre.
Quilted by Louise Haley.

Yes, those are raw edges on the four sides of each little pinwheel square and quarter-triangle square at the intersections of the blocks. And no, they are not sewn onto the quilt top after the blocks have been sewn together. They are created when the block is assembled. (The block is the same as the one used in "Radio Flyer" except for the exposed edges.)

Carrie was thinking about naming this quilt "Hobo" because it was 4-across on her mom's crossword puzzle and it sort of fit with the raw edges. But once Louise worked her magic with the quilting — turning the little raw-edge squares into the centers of flowers and quilting petals across the rest of the blocks — "Rosie's Posies" was cultivated.

YARDAGE REQUIREMENTS

Yardage is based on 43"/44" (109 cm/112 cm) wide fabric with a "usable" width of 40" (102 cm) after trimming selvages and shrinkage.

  6 yds (5.5 m) *total* of assorted light, medium, and dark pastel print fabrics

  $^1/_2$ yd (46 cm) of green print fabric for inner border

  $2^3/_8$ yds (2.2 m) of yellow print fabric for outer border

  7 yds (6.4 m) of fabric for backing

  $^7/_8$ yds (80 cm) of fabric for binding

You will also need:

  84" x 91" (213 cm x 231 cm) rectangle of batting

CUTTING OUT THE PIECES

*Follow **Rotary Cutting**, page 103, to cut fabric. All strips are cut across the width of the fabric unless otherwise noted. Borders include an extra 4" of length for "insurance" and will be trimmed after assembling quilt top center. All other measurements include $^1/_4$" seam allowances.*

From assorted light, medium, and dark pastel print fabrics:
- Cut 72 **squares** $8^3/_8$" x $8^3/_8$".
- Cut 72 squares $3^3/_8$" x $3^3/_8$". Cut squares *once* diagonally to make 144 **large triangles**.
- Cut 72 squares 3" x 3". Cut squares *once* diagonally to make 144 **small triangles**.

From green print fabric:
- Cut 7 border strips 2"w.

From yellow print fabric:
- Cut 2 *lengthwise* **top/bottom outer borders** $6^1/_2$" x $79^1/_2$".
- Cut 2 *lengthwise* **side outer borders** $6^1/_2$" x 75".

MAKING THE BLOCKS

*Follow **Piecing**, page 103, and **Pressing**, page 104 to assemble the quilt top. Use $^1/_4$" seam allowance throughout.*

1. With *right sides facing up* and raw edges matching, place 1 **large triangle** on top of 1 **square**. Stitch $^1/_4$" from long raw edge of **large triangle**. In the same manner, sew another **large triangle** to opposite corner of **square** (**Fig. 1**).

Fig. 1

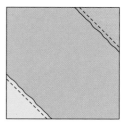

2. Repeat Step 1 to sew 1 **small triangle** to each remaining corner of **large square** to complete **Unit 1**. Make 72 **Unit 1's**.

Unit 1 (make 72)

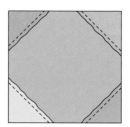

3. To reduce bulk, trim the corners of each **square** ¹/₄" from stitching lines, making sure not to cut through **triangles** (**Fig. 2**).

Fig. 2

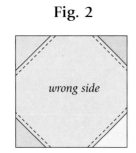

wrong side

4. Draw diagonal line (corner to corner) on wrong side of half of **Unit 1's** with line going through **large triangles**. With right sides together and matching **large triangles**, place 1 marked **Unit 1** on top of 1 unmarked **Unit 1**. Stitch seam ¹/₄" from each side of drawn line (**Fig. 3**)

Fig. 3

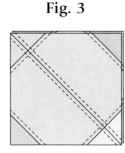

5. Cut along drawn line and open, pressing seam allowances toward one side, to make 2 **Blocks**. Make 72 **Blocks**.

Blocks (make 72)

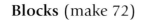
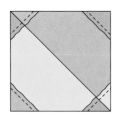
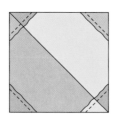

ASSEMBLING THE QUILT TOP CENTER

Pressing the seam allowances open between Blocks and Rows will reduce bulk.

1. Referring to **Quilt Top Diagram**, page 67, and rotating every other **Block**, arrange **Blocks** on floor or design wall in a manner pleasing to you. **Note:** *When the Blocks are positioned correctly, the squares at the intersections of each Block should alternate between a pinwheel and a quarter-triangle square.*

2. Sew 8 **Blocks** together, making sure **Blocks** are turned correctly, to make **Row**. Make 9 **Rows**.

3. Sew **Rows** together to make center section of quilt top.

ADDING THE BORDERS

1. Using diagonal seams, sew **border strips** together end to end (**Fig. 4**) to make 1 continuous **inner border strip**

Fig. 4

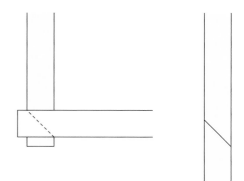

- To determine length of **side inner borders**, measure *length* of quilt top center. Cut 2 **side inner borders** from **inner border strip** to determined length. Matching centers and corners, sew **side inner borders** to quilt top center.
- To determine length of **top/bottom inner borders**, measure *width* of quilt top center (including added borders). Cut 2 **top/bottom inner borders** from **inner border strip** to determined length. Matching centers and corners, sew **top/bottom inner borders** to quilt top center.

4. Repeat Steps 2 – 3 to measure, trim, and sew **side**, **top**, and then **bottom outer borders** to quilt top.

COMPLETING THE QUILT

1. Follow **Quilting**, page 105, to mark, layer, and quilt as desired. Our quilt is machine quilted with close "pebble" quilting in the pinwheel and quarter-triangle squares for "flower centers" and large petals quilted around the flower centers.
2. Cut a 28" square of binding fabric. Follow **Binding**, page 108, to bind quilt using 2"w bias binding with mitered corners.

Quilt Top Diagram

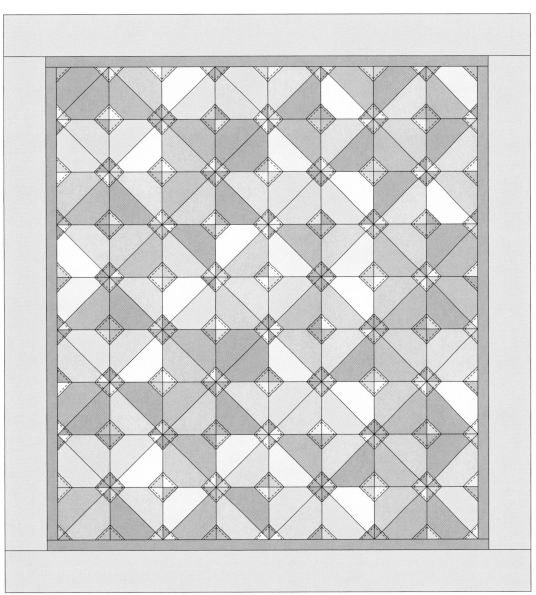

Six Degrees

Finished Quilt Size: 77" x 77" (196 cm x 196 cm)
Finished Block Size: 6" x 6" (15 cm x 15 cm)

Pieced by Carrie Nelson.
Quilted by Diane Tricka.

Carrie often names a quilt after the block or fabric line used in the quilt. While speaking with her friend, Ginger Sanchez, she commented that the name of the fabric wasn't giving her much help as it only made her think of Vincent van Gogh. Ginger laughed because van Gogh made her think of Kirk Douglas who had played him in a movie.

Don't ask Carrie how, but that somehow led to the "six degrees of separation of Kevin Bacon." She explains, "Vincent van Gogh was played by Kirk Douglas in a movie … Kirk Douglas's daughter-in-law is Catherine Zeta Jones … who was in *America's Sweetheart* with Julia Roberts … who was in *Something to Talk About* with Kyra Sedgwick … who is married to Kevin Bacon."

YARDAGE REQUIREMENTS

Yardage is based on 43"/44" (109 cm/112 cm) wide fabric with a "usable" width of 40" (102 cm) after trimming selvages and shrinkage.

  $2^3/_8$ yds (2.2 m) of tan tone-on-tone print fabric

  $2^5/_8$ yds (2.4 m) *total* of assorted cream print fabrics

  $1^1/_2$ yds (1.4 m) *total* of assorted burgundy print fabrics

  $1^1/_4$ yds (1.1 cm) *total* of assorted green print fabrics

  $^7/_8$ yds (80 cm) *total* of assorted pink print fabrics

  $7^1/_8$ yds (6.5 m) of fabric for backing

  $^7/_8$ yds (80 cm) of fabric for binding

You will also need:

  85" x 85" (216 cm x 216 cm) square of batting

CUTTING OUT THE PIECES

*Follow **Rotary Cutting**, page 103, to cut fabric. All strips are cut across the width of the fabric unless otherwise noted. Borders include an extra 4" of length for "insurance" and will be trimmed after assembling quilt top center. All other measurements include $^1/_4$" seam allowances.*

From tan tone-on-tone print fabric:
- Cut 2 strips $3^7/_8$"w. From these strips, cut 18 **medium squares** $3^7/_8$" x $3^7/_8$".
- Cut 5 strips $2^1/_2$"w. From these strips, cut 68 **smallest squares** $2^1/_2$" x $2^1/_2$".
- Cut 4 strips $3^1/_2$"w. From these strips, cut 20 **rectangles** $3^1/_2$" x $6^1/_2$".
- Cut 23 strips $1^1/_2$"w. From these strips, cut 68 **strips** $1^1/_2$" x 13".
- Cut 1 **large square** $6^1/_2$" x $6^1/_2$".
- Cut 4 **small squares** $3^1/_2$" x $3^1/_2$".

From assorted cream print fabrics:
- Cut 52 **setting squares** $6^1/_2$" x $6^1/_2$".
- Cut 8 squares $9^3/_4$" x $9^3/_4$". Cut squares *twice* diagonally to make 32 **side setting triangles**.
- Cut 2 squares $5^1/_8$" x $5^1/_8$". Cut squares *once* diagonally to make 4 **corner setting triangles**.

From assorted burgundy print fabrics:
- Cut 18 **medium squares** $3^7/_8$" x $3^7/_8$".
- For *each* of 32 **Burgundy Blocks**, cut the following pieces from 1 burgundy print fabric.
  - Cut 4 **smallest squares** $2^1/_2$" x $2^1/_2$".
  - Cut 1 **strip** $1^1/_2$" x 13".

From assorted green print fabrics:
- Cut 4 sets of 8 matching **small squares** $3^1/_2$" x $3^1/_2$".
- For *each* of 24 **Green Blocks**, cut the following pieces from 1 green print fabric.
  - Cut 4 **smallest squares** $2^1/_2$" x $2^1/_2$".
  - Cut 1 **strip** $1^1/_2$" x 13".

From assorted pink print fabrics:
- Cut 4 **largest squares** $7^1/_4$" x $7^1/_4$".
- Cut 2 **large squares** $6^1/_2$" x $6^1/_2$".
- For *each* of 12 **Pink Blocks**, cut the following pieces from 1 pink print fabric.
  - Cut 4 **smallest squares** $2^1/_2$" x $2^1/_2$".
  - Cut 1 **strip** $1^1/_2$" x 13".

MAKING THE UNITS

*Follow **Piecing**, page 103, and **Pressing**, page 104, to assemble the quilt top. Use ¹/₄" seam allowances throughout.*

Flying Geese Unit

1. With right sides together, place 1 green **small square** on 1 end of 1 tan tone-on-tone **rectangle** and stitch diagonally. Trim ¹/₄" from stitching line (**Fig. 1**). Open up and press seam allowances toward darker fabric (**Fig. 2**).

Fig. 1   **Fig. 2**

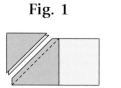

2. Place a matching green **small square** on opposite end of **rectangle**. Stitch and trim as shown in **Fig. 3**. Open up and press seam allowances toward triangle to complete **Flying Geese Unit**. Make 4 sets of 4 matching **Flying Geese Units**.

Fig. 3   **Flying Geese Unit**
(make 4 sets of 4 matching)

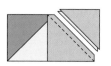   

Hourglass Unit

1. Draw diagonal line (corner to corner) on wrong side of 1 pink print **largest square**. With right sides together, place 1 marked pink **largest square** on top of 1 unmarked pink **largest square**. Stitch seam ¹/₄" from each side of drawn line (**Fig. 4**).

Fig. 4

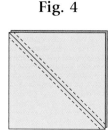

2. Cut along drawn line and press open to make 2 **Triangle-Squares**.

Triangle-Squares (make 2)

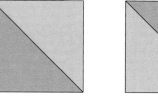 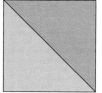

3. On wrong side of 1 **Triangle-Square**, draw diagonal line (corner to corner and perpendicular to seam).

4. Place marked **Triangle-Square** on top of unmarked **Triangle-Square** with like prints opposite each other. Stitch ¹/₄" from each side of drawn line (**Fig. 5**). Cut apart along drawn line to make 2 **Hourglass Units**; press open. Discard 1 **Hourglass Unit**.

Fig. 5

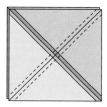

Hourglass Unit

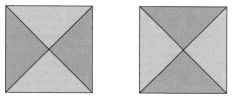

5. Repeat Steps 1 – 4 with remaining pink **largest squares** to make 2 more **Hourglass Units**. Discard 1 of these.

MAKING THE CENTER MEDALLION

The 4 Flying Geese Units around each pink large square or Hourglass Unit should be made from 1 green print. Referring to photo, page 71, for placement, arrange pieces into Rows before stitching.

1. Sew 2 tan tone-on-tone **small squares**, 2 **Flying Geese Units**, and 1 tan tone-on-tone **rectangle** together to make **Row 1**. Press seam allowances toward **small squares** and **rectangle**. Make 2 **Row 1's**.

Row 1 (make 2)

2. Sew 4 **Flying Geese Units**, 1 **Hourglass Unit**, and 1 pink **large square** together to make **Row 2**. Press seam allowances toward **Hourglass Unit** and **large square**. Make 2 **Row 2's**.

Row 2 (make 2)

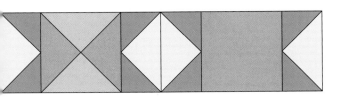

3. Arrange 2 tan tone-on-tone **rectangles**, 4 **Flying Geese Units**, and 1 tan tone-on-tone **large square** as shown in **Row 3** diagram. Sew **Flying Geese Units** together, and then **sew rectangles** and **large square** to **Flying Geese Units** to make **Row 3**. Press seam allowances toward **rectangles** and **large square**.

Row 3

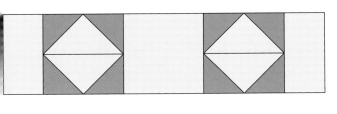

4. Sew **Rows** together to make center portion of **Center Medallion**. Press seam allowances toward **Row 2's**.

Center Medallion Assembly Diagram

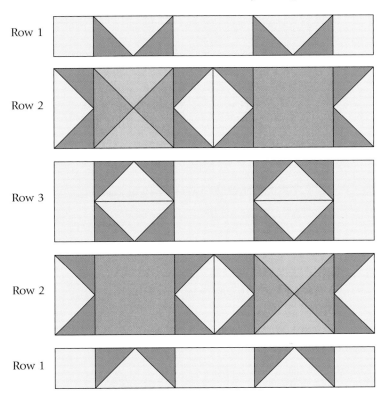

Row 1
Row 2
Row 3
Row 2
Row 1

5. Draw diagonal line (corner to corner) on wrong side of each tan tone-on-tone **medium square**. With right sides together, place 1 tan tone-on-tone **medium square** on top of 1 burgundy **medium square**. Stitch seam ¼" from each side of drawn line (**Fig. 6**).

Fig. 6

6. Cut along drawn line and press seam allowances toward darker fabric to make 2 **Triangle-Squares**. Make 36 **Triangle-Squares**.

Triangle-Squares (make 36)

7. Sew 8 **Triangle-Squares** together to make **Unit 1**. Press seam allowances open or in one direction. Make 2 **Unit 1's**.

Unit 1 (make 2)

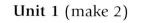

8. Sew 10 **Triangle-Squares** together to make **Unit 2**. Press seam allowances open or in one direction. Make 2 **Unit 2's**.

Unit 2 (make 2)

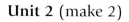

9. Sew 1 **Unit 1** to each side of center portion of **Center Medallion**. Press seam allowances toward center portion.
10. Sew 1 **Unit 2** to top and bottom of center portion to complete **Center Medallion**. Press seam allowances toward center portion.

Center Medallion

MAKING THE BLOCKS

*Each **Block** is made using the tan tone-on-tone print fabric and 1 burgundy, green, or pink print.*

1. Sew 1 tan tone-on-tone **strip** and 1 burgundy print **strip** together to make **Strip Set**. Cut **Strip Set** at $1^1/_2$" intervals to make 8 **Unit 3's**.

Strip Set   Unit 3 (make 8

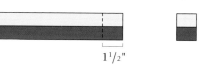

$1^1/_2$"

2. Sew 2 **Unit 3's** together to make **Unit 4**. Make 4 **Unit 4's**.

Unit 4 (make 4)

3. Sew 2 **Unit 4's** and 1 burgundy **smallest square** together to make **Unit 5**. Make 2 **Unit 5's**.

Unit 5 (make 2)

4. Sew 2 burgundy **smallest squares** and 1 tan tone-on-tone **smallest square** together to make **Unit 6**.

Unit 6

5. Sew 2 **Unit 5's** and **Unit 6** together to make **Burgundy Block**.

Burgundy Block

Repeat Steps 1 – 5 to make 32 assorted **Burgundy Blocks**, 24 assorted **Green Blocks**, and 12 assorted **Pink Blocks**.

Burgundy Block (make 32)

Green Block (make 24)

Pink Block (make 12)

ASSEMBLING THE QUILT TOP

Refer to Quilt Assembly Diagram for placement.

- Sew **Blocks**, **setting squares**, **side setting triangles**, and **corner setting triangles** together to make diagonal **Rows** for **Section I**. Sew **Rows** together to make 2 **Section I's**.
- Sew **Blocks**, **setting squares**, **side setting triangles**, and **corner setting triangles** together to make diagonal **Rows** for **Section II**. Sew **Rows** together to make 2 **Section II's**.
- Sew 2 **Section II's** and **Center Medallion** together to make **Section III**.
- Sew **Section III** and 2 **Section I's** together to complete quilt top.

COMPLETING THE QUILT

1. Follow **Quilting**, page 105, to mark, layer, and quilt as desired. *(**Note:** Stay-stitching around the quilt top approximately $^1/_8$" from the edge before quilting will help stabilize the edge and prevent any seams from separating.)* Our quilt is machine quilted with a combination of curved and straight line patterns.
2. Cut a 27" square of binding fabric. Follow **Binding**, page 108, to bind quilt using 2"w bias binding with mitered corners.

Quilt Assembly Diagram

Section I   Section II

Section II   Section I

American Pie

Finished Quilt Size: 72^1/$_2$" x 80^1/$_2$" (184 cm x 204 cm)
Finished Block Size: 8" x 8" (20 cm x 20 cm)

Pieced by Mary Dyer.
Quilted by Sharon Brooks.

No matter how they are used or what kind of pattern is chosen, there's something about feedsack prints and 1930's reproduction prints that just makes Carrie think of picnics and long summer days.

Feedsack prints seem so quintessentially American to her and the lattice formed by the blocks make her think of pie. (Which just so happens to make her think of picnics and long summer days.) So, what better name for this quilt than "American Pie"?

This quilt goes together so quickly, you'll agree it's easy as pie!

YARDAGE REQUIREMENTS

Yardage is based on 43"/44" (109 cm/112 cm) wide fabric with a "usable" width of 40" (102 cm) after trimming selvages and shrinkage.

   6^1/$_4$ yds (5.7 m) *total* of assorted print fabrics
   4^3/$_8$ yds (4 m) of cream solid fabric
   *6^3/$_4$ yds (6.2 m) of fabric for backing
   ^{7}/$_8$ yds (80 cm) of fabric for binding

You will also need:

   81" x 89" (206 cm x 226 cm) rectangle of batting
   *Yardage is based on 3 lengths of fabric, which
    allows for a larger backing for long arm quilting.
    If you are using another quilting method,
    2 lengths, or 5 yds (4.6 m), will be adequate.

CUTTING OUT THE PIECES

*Follow **Rotary Cutting**, page 103, to cut fabric. All strips are cut across the width of the fabric. All measurements include ^{1}/$_4$" seam allowances.*

From assorted print fabrics:
- Cut 144 pairs of matching **large squares** 4^1/$_2$" x 4^1/$_2$".
- Cut 72 additional **large squares** 4^1/$_2$" x 4^1/$_2$".

From cream print fabric:
- Cut 51 strips 2^3/$_4$"w. From these strips, cut 712 **small squares** 2^3/$_4$" x 2^3/$_4$".

MAKING THE BLOCKS

*Follow **Piecing**, page 103, and **Pressing**, page 104, to assemble the quilt top. Use ^{1}/$_4$" seam allowances throughout. For each **Block**, use 2 different pairs of matching large squares.*

1. With right sides together, place 1 **small square** on 1 corner of 1 **large square** and stitch diagonally (**Fig. 1**). Trim ^{1}/$_4$" from stitching line (**Fig. 2**). Open up and press seam allowances toward triangle.

Fig. 1

Fig. 2

2. Sew another **small square** to the opposite corner of **large square** as shown in **Fig. 3**. Open up and press seam allowances toward triangle to make **Unit 1**.

Fig. 3

Unit 1

3. Repeat Steps 1 – 2 using **small squares** and 72 pairs of matching **large squares** and 34 additional **large squares** to make a *total* of 178 **Unit 1's**.

4. Repeat Steps 1 – 2 using **small squares** and remaining 72 pairs of **large squares** and 34 additional **large squares**, but press seam allowances toward center of square (away from the triangles) to make a *total* of 178 **Unit 2's**.

Unit 2 (make 178)

5. For each **Block**, select 2 matching **Unit 1's** and 2 matching **Unit 2's**. Sew 1 **Unit 1** and 1 **Unit 2** together to make **Unit 3**. Press seam allowances toward **Unit 1**. Make 72 sets of 2 matching **Unit 3's** (for a total of 144 **Unit 3's**).

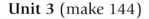

Unit 3 (make 144)

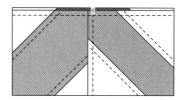

6. Sew 2 matching **Unit 3's** together to make **Block**. Before pressing, use a seam ripper to remove the la... 2 or 3 stitches (highlighted in yellow) of both seams made in Step 5 (**Fig. 4**). Press seam allowances as shown in **Fig. 5**. Make 72 **Blocks**.

Fig. 4

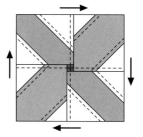

Fig. 5

Block (make 72)

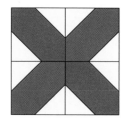

Sew 1 **Unit 1** and 1 **Unit 2** together to make **Half Block A**. Press seam allowances toward **Unit 2**. Make 18 **Half Block A's**.

Half Block A (make 18)

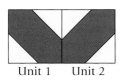

Unit 1   Unit 2

Sew 1 **Unit 1** and 1 **Unit 2** together to make **Half Block B**. Press seam allowances toward **Unit 1**. Make 16 **Half Block B's**.

Half Block B (make 16)

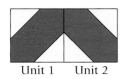

Unit 1   Unit 2

SSEMBLING THE QUILT TOP

efer to **Quilt Top Diagram** *for placement.*

Sew 8 **Half Block B's** and 2 **large squares** (1 on each end) together to make **Top Row**. Repeat to make **Bottom Row**. Press seam allowances between **Half Blocks** open or in one direction.

Sew 8 **Blocks** and 2 **Half Block A's** (1 on each end) together to make **Middle Row**. Make 9 **Middle Rows**. Press seam allowances between **Blocks** open or in one direction, alternating directions between **Rows**.

Sew **Rows** together to complete quilt top. Press seam allowances between **Rows** open or in one direction.

COMPLETING THE QUILT

1. Follow **Quilting**, page 105, to mark, layer, and quilt as desired. *(**Note:** Stay-stitching around the quilt top approximately $1/8$" from the edge before quilting will help stabilize the edge and prevent any seams from separating.)* Our quilt is machine quilted with a flower design quilted in each cream area and a feather pattern quilted in the lattice made by the assorted prints.

2. Cut a 27" square of binding fabric. Follow **Binding**, page 108, to bind quilt using 2"w bias binding with mitered corners.

Quilt Top Diagram

Tuesday Sue

Finished Quilt Size: $78^1/4$" x $78^1/4$" (199 cm x 199 cm)
Finished Block Size: 5" x 5" (13 cm x 13 cm)

Pieced by Sue Maitre.
Quilted by Sharon Brooks.

"Tuesday Sue" is Sue Maitre, who Carrie declares is a wonderful friend and quilter. Sue spends part of her year working one day a week at a very special quilt shop in Michigan. One Tuesday, a box arrived for Carrie from Sue filled with six beautiful fat-quarter bundles of homespun plaids — a grand total of 48 fat quarters!

Wanting to use every single one of the plaids, Carrie designed this quilt that is both lively and scrappy, but also a little different (a bit like Sue, according to Carrie).

Tip: *New tools and paper foundations are available for making **Triangle-Squares**. Since this quilt has 500 **Triangle-Squares** (2¹/₂" x 2¹/₂" **finished** size), it might be worth your time and effort to check these products out.*

YARDAGE REQUIREMENTS

Yardage is based on 43"/44" (109 cm/112 cm) wide fabric with a "usable" width of 40" (102 cm) after trimming selvages and shrinkage.

4³/₈ yds (4 m) *total* of assorted plaid, check, and stripe fabrics

2³/₈ yds (2.2 m) *total* of assorted light print fabrics

2³/₈ yds (2.2 m) of burgundy solid fabric

7¹/₄ yds (6.6 m) of fabric for backing

⁷/₈ yds (80 cm) of fabric for binding

You will also need:

86" x 86" (218 cm x 218 cm) square of batting

CUTTING OUT THE PIECES

*Follow **Rotary Cutting**, page 103, to cut fabric. All strips are cut across the width of the fabric. All measurements include ¹/₄" seam allowances.*

From assorted plaid, check, and stripe fabrics:

- Cut 250 **squares** 3³/₈" x 3³/₈".
- Cut 80 **strips** 1¹/₂" x 20".
- Cut 8 **rectangles** 1¹/₂" x 4¹/₂"

From assorted light print fabrics:

- Cut 250 **squares** 3³/₈" x 3³/₈".

From burgundy solid fabric:

- Cut 14 strips 5¹/₂"w. From these strips, cut 96 **setting squares** 5¹/₂" x 5¹/₂".

MAKING THE BLOCKS

*Follow **Piecing**, page 103, and **Pressing**, page 104, to assemble the quilt top. Use ¹/₄" seam allowances throughout*

1. Draw a diagonal line (corner to corner) on wrong side of each light print **square**. With right sides together, place 1 light print **square** on top of 1 plaid, check, or stripe **square**. Stitch seam ¹/₄" from each side of drawn line (**Fig. 1**).

Fig. 1

2. Cut along drawn line and press seam allowances toward darker fabric to make 1 pair of matching **Triangle-Squares**. Make 250 pairs of matching **Triangle-Squares**.

Triangle-Squares
(make 250 matching pairs)

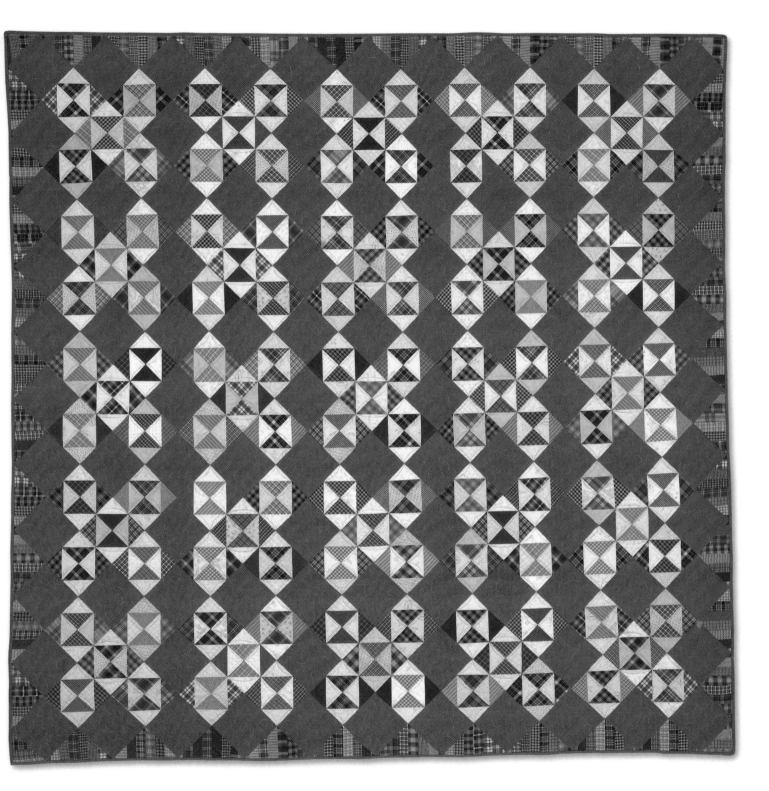

3. Randomly select 2 pairs of matching **Triangle-Squares** for 1 **Block**. Sew 1 of each pair together to make **Unit 1**. Make 2 matching **Unit 1's**. Press seam allowances toward matching **Triangle-Squares** as shown by arrows. Repeat with remaining **Triangle-Squares** to make 125 pairs of matching **Unit 1's**.

Unit 1's
(make 125 matching pairs)

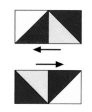

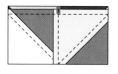

4. Sew 2 matching **Unit 1's** together to make **Block**. Before pressing, use a seam ripper to remove the last 2 or 3 stitches (highlighted in pink) of both seams made in Step 3 (**Fig. 2**). Press seam allowances as shown in **Fig. 3**. Make 125 **Blocks**.

Fig. 2   **Fig. 3**

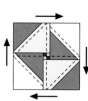

Block (make 125)

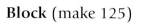

MAKING THE SETTING TRIANGLES

1. Sew 8 **strips** together in random color order to make **Strip Set**. Make 10 **Strip Sets**. Cut across **Strip Sets** at $4^1/4$" intervals to make 40 **Unit 2's**.

Strip Set (make 10)   **Unit 2** (make 40)

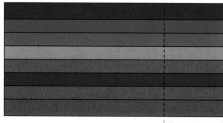

$4^1/4$"

2. Using ruler and rotary cutter, trim each **Unit 2** as shown in **Fig. 4** (from bottom corners t center of top edge) to make 40 **pieced setting triangles**.

Fig. 4

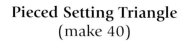

Pieced Setting Triangle
(make 40)

3. Sew 4 **rectangles** together in random color order to make **Unit 3**. Make 2 **Unit 3's**.

Unit 3 (make 2)

4. Cut 1 **Unit 3** once diagonally to make 2 **pieced corner setting triangles**. Cut remaining **Unit 3** once diagonally in the opposite direction to make 2 more **pieced corner setting triangles**.

Pieced Corner Setting Triangles
(make 4)

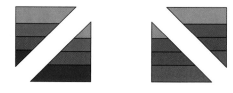

ASSEMBLING THE QUILT TOP CENTER

- Sew **pieced corner setting triangles**, **pieced setting triangles**, **setting squares**, and **Blocks** together into diagonal **Rows**, carefully following **Quilt Assembly Diagram** for placement and **Block** orientation. Press seam allowances toward **setting squares** or toward middle **Block** when 3 **Blocks** are together.
- Sew **Rows** together, pressing seam allowances toward even numbered **Rows**. Trim edges of quilt top if needed, *leaving $^1/_4$" seam allowance beyond points.*

COMPLETING THE QUILT

1. Follow **Quilting**, page 105, to mark, layer, and quilt as desired. (*Note: Stay-stitching around the quilt top approximately $^1/_8$" from the edge before quilting will help stabilize the edge and prevent any seams from separating.*) Our quilt is machine quilted with an all-over leaf and vine pattern.
2. Cut a 28" square of binding fabric. Follow **Binding**, page 108, to bind quilt using 2"w bias binding with mitered corners.

Quilt Assembly Diagram

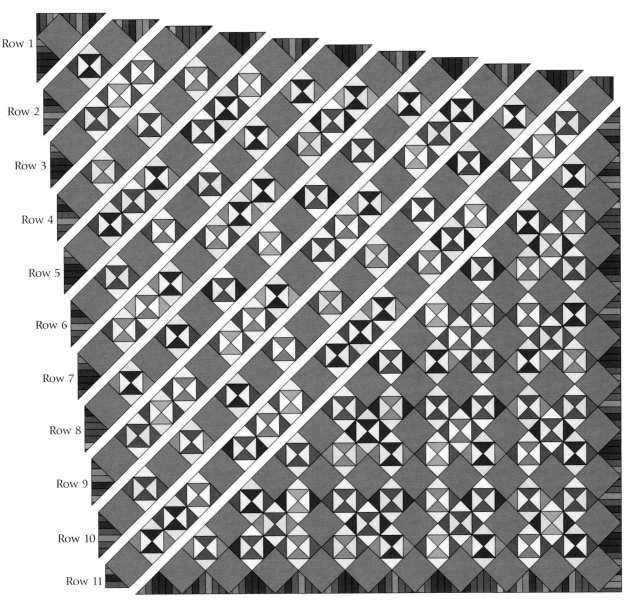

Row 1
Row 2
Row 3
Row 4
Row 5
Row 6
Row 7
Row 8
Row 9
Row 10
Row 11

87

Sweet Emma Rose

Finished Quilt Size: 78" x 94¹/₂" (198 cm x 240 cm)

Pieced by Judy Adams.
Quilted by Sandra Strunk.

"*Sweet* Emma Rose" was inspired by an antique quilt that Carrie saw many years ago, although that one had a much stronger light/dark contrast. While she liked the very strong horizontal chevron lines created by alternating the light and the dark, she wanted something softer and less planned. Also, she wanted to use diamonds that were large enough to accommodate some of the wonderful large floral prints that are so prevalent today.

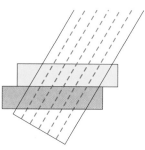

Tip: Because this quilt is made with strip piecing, it's fast and easy! You will need a 6" x 24" ruler with a 60° angle marking to cut the proper angle on the strip sets.

YARDAGE REQUIREMENTS

Yardage is based on 43"/44" (109 cm/112 cm) wide fabric with a "usable" width of 40" (102 cm) after trimming selvages and shrinkage.

- 4 yds (3.7 m) *total* of assorted light (white and yellow) print fabrics
- 4 yds (3.7 m) *total* of assorted dark (green, pink, and lilac) print fabrics
- $5/8$ yd (57 cm) of pink stripe for inner border
- $2^7/8$ yd (2.6 m) of yellow floral for outer border
- $7^1/4$ yds (6.6 m) of fabric for backing
- 1 yd (91 cm) of binding fabric

You will also need:

- 86" x 103" (218 cm x 262 cm) rectangle of batting

CUTTING OUT THE PIECES

Follow Rotary Cutting, page 103, to cut fabric. All strips are cut across the width of the fabric unless otherwise noted. Borders include an extra 4" of length for "insurance" and will be trimmed after assembling quilt top center. All other measurements include $1/4$" seam allowances.

From assorted light print fabrics*:

- Cut 22 **strips** 5"w.
- Cut 7 **rectangles** $5^5/8$" x $3^1/4$".

From assorted dark print fabrics*:

- Cut 22 **strips** 5"w.
- Cut 7 **rectangles** $5^5/8$" x $3^1/4$".

From pink stripe fabric:

- Cut 10 **inner border strips** $1^3/4$"w.

From yellow floral fabric:

- Cut 2 *lengthwise* **side outer borders** $6^1/2$" x $98^1/2$".
- Cut 2 *lengthwise* **top/bottom outer borders** $6^1/2$" x 82".

*The **four-patch diamonds** are optional. There are 12 in our quilt. You may include as many as you like—or leave them out completely. For *each* **four-patch diamond**, you will need to cut 1 **small strip** $2^3/4$" x 10" from the assorted light print fabrics *and* 1 **small strip** $2^3/4$" x 10" from the assorted dark print fabrics.

MAKING THE FOUR-PATCH DIAMONDS (OPTIONAL)

Follow Piecing, page 103, and Pressing, page 104, to make quilt top. Use $1/4$" seam allowances throughout.

1. Sew 1 light **small strip** and 1 dark **small strip** together lengthwise, offsetting **strips** by $1^1/2$" to make **Strip Set A**. Press seam allowances toward dark strip.

Strip Set A

2. Aligning 60° line on ruler (shown in pink) with bottom edge of **Strip Set A**, trim right edge (**Fig. 1**)

Fig. 1

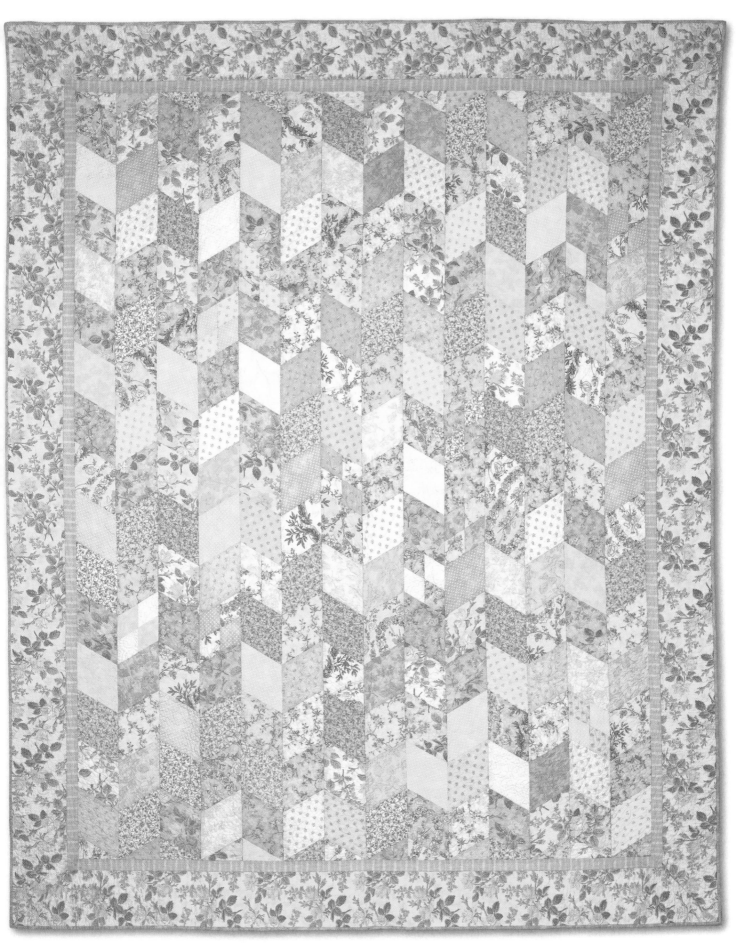

3. Rotate **Strip Set A** so that trimmed edge is on left. Aligning 60° line on ruler with bottom edge of **Strip Set A**, place ruler on **Strip Set A** so that the 2³/₄" mark on ruler is aligned with trimmed edge (**Fig. 2**). Cut on right side of ruler to make 1 **Unit 1**. Move ruler to right and align 2³/₄" mark with cut edge. Cut on right side of ruler to and make a second **Unit 1**.

Fig. 2   **Unit 1** (make 2)

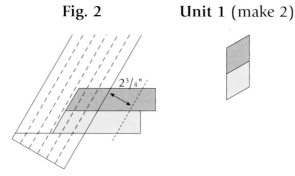

4. Sew 2 **Unit 1's** together to make **Four-Patch Diamond**. Press seam allowances in one direction. Make as many **Four-Patch Diamonds** as desired.

Four-Patch Diamond

MAKING THE DIAMOND UNITS

1. With dark **strip** on top and alternating dark and light **strips**, sew 4 **strips** together lengthwise, offsetting **strips** by 3", to make **Strip Set B**. Press seam allowances toward dark strips. Make 4 **Strip Set B's**.

Strip Set B (make 4)

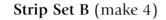

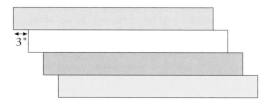

2. Aligning 60° line on ruler with bottom edge of **Strip Set B**, trim right edge (**Fig. 3**).

Fig. 3

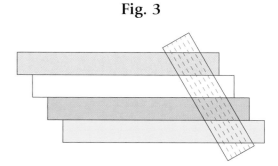

3. Rotate **Strip Set B** so that trimmed edge is on left. Aligning 60° line on ruler with bottom edge of **Strip Set B**, place ruler on **Strip Set B** so that the 5" mark on ruler is aligned with trimmed edge (**Fig. 4**). Cut on right side of ruler to make 1 **Unit 2**. Moving ruler to right, aligning 5" mark with cut edge, and cutting on right side of ruler, continue making **Unit 2's**. Repeat with remaining **Strip Set B's** to make a *total* of 21 **Unit 2's**.

Fig. 4   **Unit 2** (make 21)

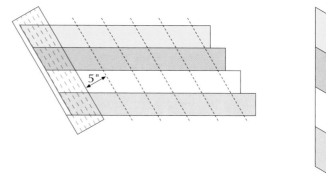

4. With dark **strip** on top and alternating dark and light **strips**, sew 3 **strips** together lengthwise, offsetting **strips** by 3", to make **Strip Set C**. Press seam allowances toward dark strips. Make 2 **Strip Set C's**.

Strip Set C (make 2)

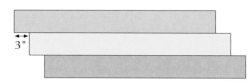

Follow Steps 2 – 3 to make 7 **Unit 3's** from **Strip Set C's**.

Unit 3 (make 7)

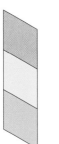

With light **strip** on top and alternating light and dark **strips**, sew 4 **strips** together lengthwise, offsetting **strips** by 3", to make **Strip Set D**. Press seam allowances toward dark strips. Make 4 **Strip Set D's**.

Strip Set D (make 4)

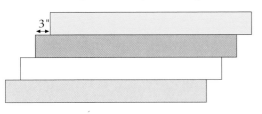

Aligning 60° line on ruler with bottom edge of **Strip Set D**, trim right edge (**Fig. 5**).

Fig. 5

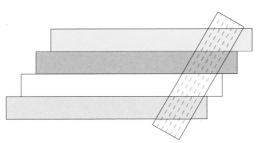

8. Rotate **Strip Set D** so that trimmed edge is on left. Aligning 60° line on ruler with bottom edge of **Strip Set D**, place ruler on **Strip Set D** so that the 5" mark on ruler is aligned with trimmed edge (**Fig. 6**). Cut on right side of ruler to make 1 **Unit 4**. Moving ruler to right, aligning 5" mark with cut edge, and cutting on right side of ruler, continue making **Unit 4's**. Repeat with remaining **Strip Set D's** to make a *total* of 21 **Unit 2's**.

Fig. 6   **Unit 4** (make 21)

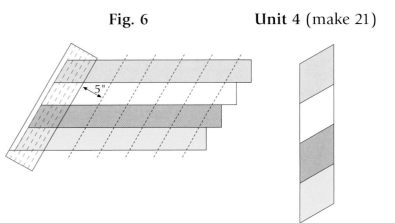
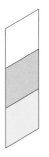

9. With light **strip** on top and alternating light and dark **strips**, sew 3 **strips** together lengthwise, offsetting **strips** by 3", to make **Strip Set E**. Press seam allowances toward dark strip. Make 2 **Strip Set E's**.

Strip Set E (make 2)

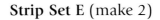

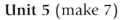

10. Follow Steps 7 – 8 to make 7 **Unit 5's** from **Strip Set E's**.

Unit 5 (make 7)

11. Cut 7 light **rectangles** *once* diagonally as shown in **Fig. 7** to make 14 **triangle A's**.

Fig. 7

Triangle A's (make 14)

12. Cut 7 dark **rectangles** *once* diagonally as shown in **Fig. 8** to make 14 **triangle B's** (notice that angle of cut is different from **triangle A's**).

Fig. 8

Triangle B's (make 14)

ASSEMBLING THE QUILT TOP CENTER

Refer to **Quilt Top Diagram***, page 95, for placement.* **Note:** *If including* **Four-Patch Diamonds***, randomly replace large diamonds with* **Four-Patch Diamonds** *while constructing* **Rows***. Separate seams within* **Diamond Units** *to insert* **Four-Patch Diamonds** *as desired.*

1. Sew 3 **Unit 2's** and 1 **Unit 3** together to form long strip. Sew 1 **Triangle A** to top end of strip and 1 **Triangle A** to bottom end to make vertical **Row A**. Press seam allowances toward dark fabrics. Make 7 **Row A's**.

2. Sew 3 **Unit 4's** and 1 **Unit 5** together to form long strip. Sew 1 **Triangle B** to top end of strip and 1 **Triangle B** to bottom end to make vertical **Row B**. Press seam allowances toward dark fabrics. Make 7 **Row B's**.

3. Beginning with **Row A** and alternating **Row A's** and **Row B's**, sew **Rows** together to make **Quilt Top Center**. Press seam allowances in one direction.

ADDING THE BORDERS

1. Using diagonal seams, sew **border strips** together end to end (**Fig. 8**) to make 1 continuous **inner border strip**.

Fig. 9

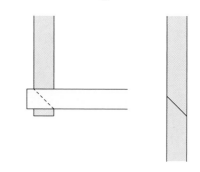

2. From **inner border strip**, cut 2 **side inner borders** $98^{1}/_{2}$"l and 2 **top/bottom inner borders** 82"l.

3. Sew 1 **side inner border** and 1 **side outer bord** together lengthwise to make 1 **side border**. Mak 2 **side borders**.

4. Sew 1 **top/bottom inner border** and **top/bottom outer border** together lengthwise to make **top border**. Repeat to make **bottom border**.

5. Mark the center of each edge of quilt top. Mark the center of inner edge of each **border**. Measure across center of quilt top. Beginning at center of **top border**, measure $^{1}/_{2}$ the width of the quilt top in both directions and mark.

6. Matching raw edges and marks on **top border** with center and corners of quilt top and easing in any fullness, pin **top border** to quilt top. Sew to border to quilt top, beginning and ending exactl $^{1}/_{4}$" from each corner of quilt top. Backstitch at beginning and ending of stitching to reinforce.

7. Repeat Steps 5 – 6 to sew **bottom** and then **side borders** to quilt top.

Fold 1 corner of quilt top diagonally with right sides together and matching edges. Aligning ruler with fold, use ruler to mark stitching line as shown in **Fig. 10**. Sew on drawn line, backstitching at beginning and ending of stitching. Turn mitered corner right side up. Check to make sure corner will lie flat with no gaps or puckers. Trim seam allowances to $^1/_4$" and press to one side. Repeat for other corners.

Fig. 10

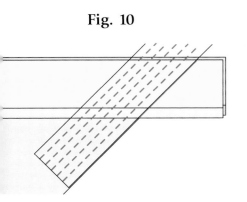

COMPLETING THE QUILT

1. Follow **Quilting**, page 105, to mark, layer, and quilt as desired. Our quilt is machine quilted with an all-over feather pattern.
2. Cut a 29" square of binding fabric. Follow **Binding**, page 108, to bind quilt using 2"w bias binding with mitered corners.

Quilt Top Diagram

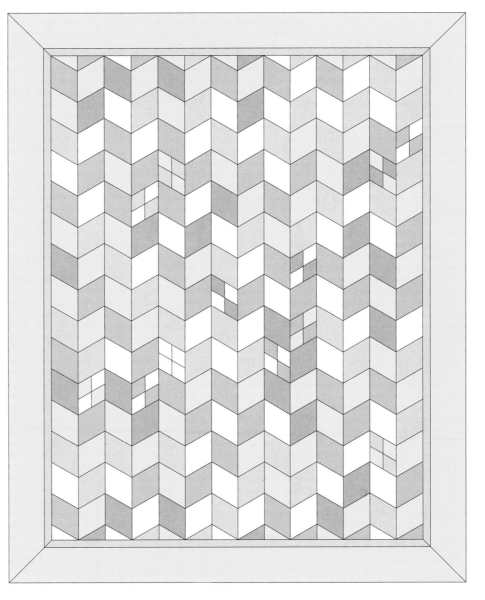

Jelly Bellies

Finished Quilt Size: 73" x 79¹/₂" (185 cm x 202 cm)
Finished Block Size: 4¹/₂" x 4¹/₂" (11 cm x 11 cm)

Pieced by Judy Adams.
Quilted by Louise Haley.

Some of the best quilts are also the simplest. And it doesn't get much easier than snowball blocks!

Whether you start with a wonderful collection, fat quarters you've chosen yourself, or the contents of your scrap bag, the only hard part about this quilt is deciding which fabrics to use. The good news is that you can use as many fabrics as you like! Just think in terms of "light" and "dark."

The name for this quilt was a long time coming. Carrie and Judy couldn't come up with anything that they both loved. They couldn't even come up with something that one of them "liked." Carrie doesn't know if it was fatigue, desperation, or hunger, but while looking at a picture of the quilt, she thought it looked like a jar of jelly beans.

YARDAGE REQUIREMENTS

Yardage is based on 43"/44" (109 cm/112 cm) wide fabric with a "usable" width of 40" (102 cm) after trimming selvages and shrinkage.

- $4^7/_8$ yds (4.5 m) *total* of assorted dark print fabrics
- $3^3/_8$ yds (3.1 m) *total* of assorted light print fabrics
- $5/_8$ yd (57 cm) of tan print fabric
- *$6^3/_4$ yds (6.2 m) of fabric for backing
- $7/_8$ yds (80 cm) of fabric for binding

You will also need:

- 81" x 88" (206 cm x 224 cm) rectangle of batting
- *Yardage is based on 3 lengths of fabric, which allows for a larger backing for long arm quilting. If you are using another quilting method, 2 lengths, or 5 yds (4.6 m) will be adequate.

CUTTING OUT THE PIECES

*Follow **Rotary Cutting**, page 103, to cut fabric. All strips are cut across the width of the fabric. All measurements include $1/_4$" seam allowances.*

From assorted dark print fabrics:
- Cut 48 **strips** 2" x 20".
- Cut 110 **large squares** 5" x 5".
- Cut 398 **small squares** $1^3/_4$" x $1^3/_4$".
- Cut 4 **corner border squares** 5" x 5".

From assorted light print fabrics:
- Cut 16 **strips** 2" x 20".
- Cut 90 **large squares** 5" x 5".
- Cut 398 **small squares** $1^3/_4$" x $1^3/_4$".

From tan print fabric:
- Cut 2 strips $7^5/_8$"w. From these strips, cut 10 squares $7^5/_8$" x $7^5/_8$". Cut squares *twice* diagonally to make 40 **setting triangles**. (You will use 38 and have 2 left over.)
- Cut 2 squares $4^1/_8$" x $4^1/_8$". Cut squares *once* diagonally to make 4 **corner setting triangles**.

MAKING THE BLOCKS

*Follow **Piecing**, page 103, and **Pressing**, page 104, to assemble the quilt top. Use $1/_4$" seam allowances throughout.*

1. With right sides together, place 1 light print **small square** on 1 corner of 1 dark print **large square** and stitch diagonally (**Fig. 1**). Trim $1/_4$" from stitching line (**Fig. 2**). Open up and press, pressing seam allowances toward **large square**.

Fig. 1   **Fig. 2**

2. Continue adding assorted light print **small squares** to corners of dark print **large square** as shown in **Fig. 3**. Open up and press seam allowances toward **large square** to complete **Block A**. Make 72 **Block A's**.

Fig. 3   **Block A** (make 72)

3. Repeat Steps 1 – 2 using dark print **small squares** and light print **large squares**, pressing seam allowances toward triangles, to make 90 **Block B's**.

Block B (make 90)

4. In the same manner, sew light print **small squares** to 3 corners of dark print **large squares**, pressing seam allowances toward **large squares**, to make 34 **Block C's**.

Block C (make 34)

5. In the same manner, sew light print **small squares** to 2 adjacent corners of dark print **large squares**, pressing seam allowances toward **large squares**, to make 4 **Block D's**.

Block D (make 4)

6. In the same manner, sew 1 dark print **small square** to right-angled corner of 1 **setting triangle**, pressing seam allowances toward small triangle, to make **pieced setting triangle**. Make 38 **pieced setting triangles**.

Pieced Setting Triangle (make 38)

ASSEMBLING THE QUILT TOP CENTER

*Refer to **Quilt Assembly Diagram**, page 101, for placement. Press seam allowances toward **Block B's** and **pieced setting triangles**.*

1. Sew 2 **pieced setting triangles**, 1 **corner setting triangle**, and 1 **Block D** together to make **Row 1**. Make 2 **Row 1's**.

Row 1 (make 2)

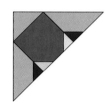

2. **Rows 2 – 9** are pieced diagonally, with 1 **Block C** and 1 **pieced setting triangle** at each end. **Block A's** and **Block B's** are alternated. Sew 2 *each* of **Rows 2 – 9**.
3. Sew 1 **corner setting triangle**, 1 **Block D**, 9 **Block B's**, 8 **Block A's**, 1 **Block C**, and 1 **pieced setting triangle** together to make **Row 10**. Make 2 **Row 10's**.
4. Sew **Rows** together to complete quilt top center. Press seam allowances in one direction.

ADDING THE BORDERS

1. Sew 6 dark print **strips** and 2 light print **strips** together lengthwise in random color order to make **Strip Set**. Press seam allowances in one direction. Make 8 **Strip Sets**. Cut across **Strip Sets** at 5" intervals to make 24 **Unit 1's**.

Strip Set
(make 8)

Unit 1
(make 24)

5"

Sew 6 **Unit 1's** together to make **border**. Make 4 **borders**.

To determine length of **side borders**, measure *length* of quilt top center. Remove rectangles and/or make a few seams between rectangles larger or smaller to make length of **side borders** equal to determined length. Do not sew borders to quilt top center at this time.

To determine length of **top/bottom borders**, measure *width* of quilt top center. Remove rectangles and/or make a few seams between rectangles larger or smaller to make length of **top/bottom borders** equal to determined length. Do not sew borders to quilt top center at this time.

Sew 1 **corner border square** to *each* end of **top** and **bottom borders**.

Matching centers and corners, sew **side**, **top**, and then **bottom borders** to quilt top center.

COMPLETING THE QUILT

1. Follow **Quilting**, page 105, to mark, layer, and quilt as desired. *(Note: Stay-stitching around the quilt top approximately $1/8$" from the edge before quilting will help stabilize the edge and prevent any seams from separating.)* Our quilt is machine quilted with an all-over leaf and vine pattern.

2. Cut a 27" square of binding fabric. Follow **Binding**, page 108, to bind quilt using 2"w bias binding with mitered corners.

Quilt Assembly Diagram

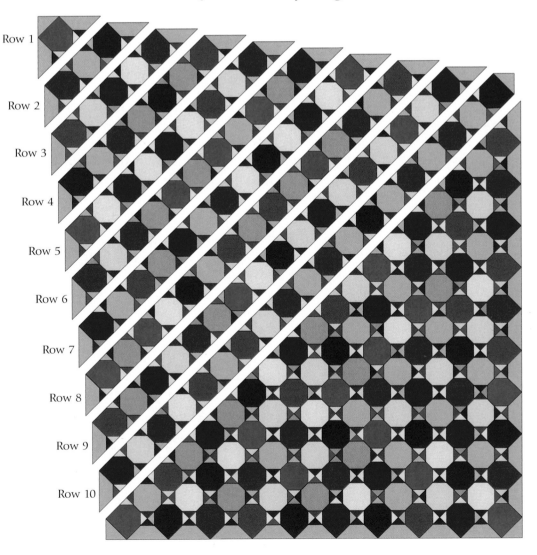

Row 1
Row 2
Row 3
Row 4
Row 5
Row 6
Row 7
Row 8
Row 9
Row 10

General Instructions

To make your quilting easier and more enjoyable, we encourage you to carefully read all of the general instructions, study the color photographs, and familiarize yourself with the individual project instructions before beginning a project.

FABRICS

SELECTING FABRICS

Choose high-quality, medium-weight 100% cotton fabrics. All-cotton fabrics hold a crease better, fray less, and are easier to quilt than cotton/polyester blends.

Yardage requirements listed for each project are based on 43"/44" wide fabric with a "usable" width of 40" after shrinkage and trimming selvages. Actual usable width will probably vary slightly from fabric to fabric. Our recommended yardage lengths should be adequate for occasional re-squaring of fabric when many cuts are required.

PREPARING FABRICS

We recommend that all fabrics be washed, dried, and pressed before cutting. If fabrics are not pre-washed, washing the finished quilt will cause shrinkage and give it a more "antiqued" look and feel. Bright and dark colors, which may run, should always be washed before cutting. After washing and drying fabric, fold lengthwise with wrong sides together and matching selvages.

ROTARY CUTTING

otary cutting has brought speed and accuracy
quiltmaking by allowing quilters to easily
t strips of fabric and then cut those strips
to smaller pieces.

Place fabric on work surface with fold closest to you.

Cut all strips from the selvage-to-selvage width of the fabric unless otherwise indicated in project instructions.

Square left edge of fabric using rotary cutter and rulers (**Figs. 1 – 2**).

Fig. 1

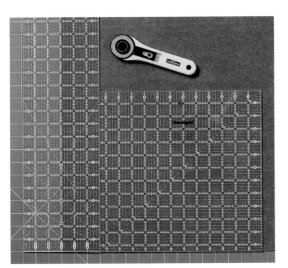

Fig. 2

- To cut each strip required for a project, place ruler over cut edge of fabric, aligning desired marking on ruler with cut edge; make cut (**Fig. 3**).

Fig. 3

- When cutting several strips from a single piece of fabric, it is important to make sure that cuts remain at a perfect right angle to the fold; square fabric as needed.

PIECING

Precise cutting, followed by accurate piecing, will ensure that all pieces of quilt top fit together well.

HAND PIECING

- Use ruler and sharp fabric marking pencil to draw all seam lines onto back of cut pieces.

- Matching right sides, pin two pieces together, using pins to mark corners.

- Use Running Stitch to sew pieces together along drawn line, backstitching at beginning and end of seam.

- Do not extend stitches into seam allowances.

- Run five or six stitches onto needle before pulling needle through fabric.

- To add stability, backstitch every $3/4$" to 1".

MACHINE PIECING

- Set sewing machine stitch length for approximately 11 stitches per inch.

- Use neutral-colored general-purpose sewing thread (not quilting thread) in needle and in bobbin.

- An accurate $1/4$" seam allowance is *essential*. Presser feet that are $1/4$" wide are available for most sewing machines.

- When piecing, always place pieces right sides together and match raw edges; pin if necessary.

- Chain piecing saves time and will usually result in more accurate piecing.

- Trim away points of seam allowances that extend beyond edges of sewn pieces.

Sewing Strip Sets

When there are several strips to assemble into a strip set, first sew strips together into pairs, then sew pairs together to form strip set. To help avoid distortion, sew seams in opposite directions (**Fig. 4**). Take special care not to stretch outer strips.

Fig. 4

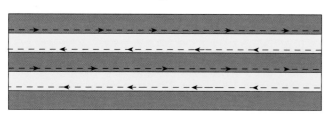

Sewing Across Seam Intersections

When sewing across intersection of two seams, place pieces right sides together and match seams exactly, making sure seam allowances are pressed in opposite directions (**Fig. 5**) or pressed open.

Fig. 5

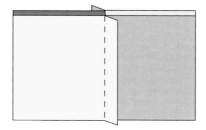

Sewing Sharp Points

To ensure sharp points when joining triangular or diagonal pieces, stitch across the center of the "X" (shown in pink) formed on wrong side by previous seams (**Fig. 6**).

Fig. 6

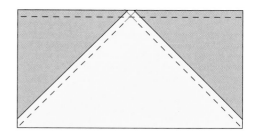

PRESSING

- Use steam iron set on "Cotton" for all pressing.

- Press after sewing each seam.

- In most cases, seam allowances should be pressed to one side, usually toward the darker fabric. However, with better fabrics, thread, and machine piecing, pressing seams open, especially between blocks, has become more commonplace. Pressing seams open may reduce bulk and make points sharper. Pressing suggestions have been provided with the individual projects in this book.

- To prevent dark fabric seam allowance from showing through light fabric, trim darker seam allowance slightly narrower than lighter seam allowance.

- To press long seams, such as those in long strip sets, without curving or other distortion, lay strips across width of the ironing board.

QUILTING

Quilting holds the three layers (top, batting, and backing) of the quilt together and can be done by hand or machine. Because marking, layering, and quilting are interrelated and may be done in different orders depending on circumstances, please read entire the **Quilting** section, pages 105-108, before beginning a project.

TYPES OF QUILTING DESIGNS

In the Ditch Quilting
Quilting along seamlines or along edges of appliquéd pieces is called "in the ditch" quilting. This type of quilting should be done on side **opposite** seam allowance and does not have to be marked.

Outline Quilting
Quilting a consistent distance, usually 1/4", from seam or appliqué is called "outline" quilting. Outline quilting may be marked, or 1/4" masking tape may be placed along seamlines for quilting guide. (Do not leave tape on quilt longer than necessary, since it may leave an adhesive residue.)

Motif Quilting
Quilting a design, such as a feathered wreath, is called "motif" quilting. This type of quilting should be marked before basting quilt layers together.

Echo Quilting
Quilting that follows the outline of an appliquéd or pieced design with two or more parallel lines is called "echo" quilting. This type of quilting does not need to be marked.

Channel Quilting
Quilting with straight, parallel lines is called "channel" quilting. This type of quilting may be marked or stitched using a guide.

Crosshatch Quilting
Quilting straight lines in a grid pattern is called "crosshatch" quilting. Lines may be stitched parallel to edges of quilt or stitched diagonally. This type of quilting may be marked or stitched using a guide.

Meandering Quilting
Quilting in random curved lines and swirls is called "meandering" quilting. Quilting lines should not cross or touch each other. This type of quilting does not need to be marked.

Stipple Quilting
Meandering quilting that is very closely spaced is called "stipple" quilting. Stippling will flatten the area quilted and is often stitched in background areas to raise appliquéd or pieced designs. This type of quilting does not need to be marked.

MARKING QUILTING LINES
Quilting lines may be marked using fabric marking pencils, chalk markers, water- or air-soluble pens, or lead pencils.

Simple quilting designs may be marked with chalk or chalk pencil after basting. A small area may be marked, then quilted, before moving to next area to be marked. Intricate designs should be marked before basting using a more durable marker.

Caution: Pressing may permanently set some marks. **Test** different markers **on scrap fabric** to find one that marks clearly and can be thoroughly removed.

A wide variety of pre-cut quilting stencils, as well as entire books of quilting patterns, are available. Using a stencil makes it easier to mark intricate or repetitive designs.

To make a stencil from a pattern, center template plastic over pattern and use a permanent marker to trace pattern onto plastic. Use a craft knife with single or double blade to cut channels along traced lines (**Fig. 7**).

Fig. 7

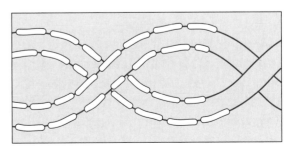

PREPARING THE BACKING

To allow for slight shifting of quilt top during quilting, backing should be approximately 4" larger on all sides, especially for quilts which will be quilted on a long arm machine. Less fabric (2" to 3" larger on all sides) is adequate for quilts which will be hand quilted or quilted on a regular sewing machine. In some cases, this will allow you to avoid purchasing an extra length of fabric. Yardage requirements listed for quilt backings are calculated for 43"/44"w fabric. Using 90"w or 108"w fabric for the backing of a bed-sized quilt may eliminate piecing. To piece a backing using 43"/44"w fabric, use the following instructions.

1. Measure length and width of quilt top; add 8" to each measurement.
2. If determined width is 79" or less, cut backing fabric into two lengths slightly longer than determined **length** measurement. Trim selvages. Place lengths with right sides facing and sew long edges together, forming tube (**Fig. 8**). Match seams and press along one fold (**Fig. 9**). Cut along pressed fold to form single piece (**Fig. 10**).

Fig. 8   **Fig. 9**   **Fig. 10**

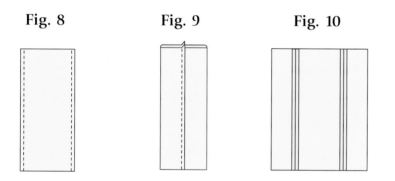

3. If determined width is more than 79", it may require less fabric yardage if the backing is pieced horizontally. Divide determined **length** measurement by 40" to determine how many widths will be needed. Cut required number of widths the determined **width** measurement. Trim selvages. Sew long edges together to form single piece.
4. Trim backing to size determined in Step 1; press seam allowances open.

CHOOSING THE BATTING

The appropriate batting will make quilting easier. For fine hand quilting, choose low-loft batting. All cotton or cotton/polyester blend battings work well for machine quilting because the cotton helps "grip" quilt layers. If a quilt is to be tied, a high-loft batting, sometimes called extra-loft or fat batting, may be used to make the quilt "fluffy."

Types of batting include cotton, polyester, cotton/polyester blend, wool, cotton/wool blend, and silk. When selecting batting, refer to package labels for characteristics and care instructions. Batting should be cut same size as prepared backing.

ASSEMBLING THE QUILT

1. Examine wrong side of quilt top closely; trim any seam allowances and clip any threads that may show through front of the quilt. Press quilt top, being careful not to "set" any marked quilting lines.
2. Place backing **wrong** side up on flat surface. Use masking tape to tape edges of backing to surface. Place batting on top of backing fabric. Smooth batting gently, being careful not to stretch or tear. Center quilt top **right** side up on batting.
3. If hand quilting, begin in center and work toward outer edges to hand baste all layers together. Use long stitches and place basting lines approximately 4" apart (**Fig. 11**). Smooth fullness or wrinkles toward outer edges.

Fig. 11

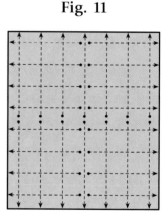

4. If machine quilting, use 1" rustproof safety pins to "pin-baste" all layers together, spacing pins approximately 4" apart. Begin at center and work toward outer edges to secure all layers. If possible, place pins away from areas that will be quilted, although pins may be removed as needed when quilting.

AND QUILTING

The quilting stitch is a basic running stitch that forms a broken line on quilt top and backing. Stitches on quilt top and backing should be straight and equal in length.

Secure center of quilt in hoop or frame. Check quilt top and backing to make sure they are smooth. To help prevent puckers, always begin quilting in the center of quilt and work toward outside edges.

Thread needle with 18" - 20" length of quilting thread; knot one end. Using thimble, insert needle into quilt top and batting approximately $^1/_2$" from quilting line. Bring needle up on quilting line (**Fig. 12**); when knot catches on quilt top, give thread a quick, short pull to "pop" knot through fabric into batting (**Fig. 13**).

Fig. 12	Fig. 13

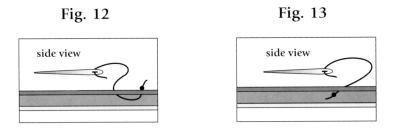

Holding needle with sewing hand and placing other hand underneath quilt, use thimble to push tip of needle down through all layers. As soon as needle touches finger underneath, use that finger to push tip of needle only back up through layers to top of quilt. (The amount of needle showing above fabric determines length of quilting stitch.) Referring to **Fig. 14**, rock needle up and down, taking three to six stitches before bringing needle and thread completely through layers. Check back of quilt to make sure stitches are going through all layers. If necessary, make one stitch at a time when quilting through seam allowances or along curves and corners.

Fig. 14

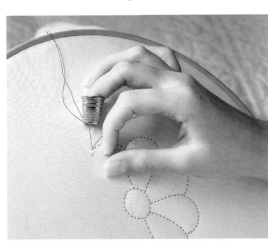

4. At end of thread, knot thread close to fabric and "pop" knot into batting; clip thread close to fabric.

5. Move hoop as often as necessary. Thread may be left dangling and picked up again after returning to that part of quilt.

MACHINE QUILTING METHODS

Use general-purpose thread in bobbin. Do not use quilting thread. Thread the needle of machine with general-purpose thread or transparent monofilament thread to make quilting blend with quilt top fabrics. Use decorative thread, such as a metallic or contrasting-color general-purpose thread, to make quilting lines stand out more.

Straight-Line Quilting

The term "straight-line" is somewhat deceptive, since curves (especially gentle ones) as well as straight lines can be stitched with this technique.

1. Set stitch length for six to ten stitches per inch and attach walking foot to sewing machine.

2. Determine which section of quilt will have longest continuous quilting line, oftentimes area from center top to center bottom. Roll up and secure each edge of quilt to help reduce the bulk, keeping fabrics smooth.

3. Begin stitching on longest quilting line, using very short stitches for the first $^1/_4$" to "lock" quilting. Stitch across project, using one hand on each side of walking foot to slightly spread fabric and to guide fabric through machine. Lock stitches at end of quilting line.

4. Continue machine quilting, stitching longer quilting lines first to stabilize quilt before moving on to other areas.

Free-Motion Quilting

Free-motion quilting may be free form or may follow a marked pattern.

1. Attach darning foot to sewing machine and lower or cover feed dog.

2. Position quilt under darning foot; lower foot. Holding top thread, take a stitch and pull bobbin thread to top of quilt. To "lock" beginning of quilting line, hold top and bobbin threads while making three to five stitches in place.

3. Use one hand on each side of darning foot to slightly spread fabric and to move fabric through the machine. Even stitch length is achieved by using smooth, flowing hand motion and steady machine speed. Slow machine speed and fast hand movement will create long stitches. Fast machine speed and slow hand movement will create short stitches. Move quilt sideways, back and forth, in a circular motion, or in a random motion to create desired designs; do not rotate quilt. Lock stitches at end of each quilting line.

BINDING

Binding encloses the raw edges of a quilt. Because of its stretchiness, bias binding works well for binding projects with curves or rounded corners and tends to lie smooth and flat in any given circumstance. Binding may also be cut from straight lengthwise or crosswise grain of fabric.

MAKING CONTINUOUS BIAS STRIP BINDING

Bias strips for binding can simply be cut and pieced to desired length. However, when a long length of binding is needed, the "continuous" method is quick and accurate.

1. Cut square from binding fabric the size indicated in project instructions. Cut square in half diagonally to make two triangles.

2. With right sides together and using ¹/₄" seam allowance, sew triangles together (**Fig. 15**); press seam allowances open.

Fig. 15

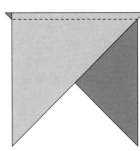

3. On wrong side of fabric, draw lines 2" apart (**Fig. 16**). Cut off any remaining fabric less than this width.

Fig. 16

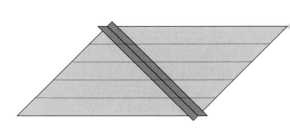

4. With right sides inside, bring short edges together to form tube; match raw edges so that first drawn line of top section meets second drawn line of bottom section (**Fig. 17**).

Fig. 17

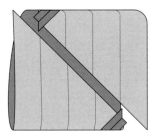

5. Carefully pin edges together by inserting pins through drawn lines at point where drawn lines intersect, making sure pins go through intersections on both sides. Using ¹/₄" seam allowance, sew edges together; press seam allowances open.

To cut continuous strip, begin cutting along first drawn line (**Fig. 18**). Continue cutting along drawn line around tube.

Fig. 18

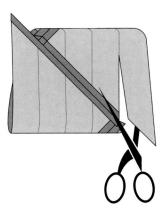

- Trim ends of bias strip square.
- Matching wrong sides and raw edges, carefully press bias strip in half lengthwise to complete binding.

ATTACHING BINDING WITH MITERED CORNERS

- Press one end of binding diagonally.
- Beginning with one end near center on bottom edge of quilt, lay binding around quilt to make sure that seams in binding will not end up at a corner. Adjust placement if necessary. Matching raw edges of binding to raw edge of quilt top, pin binding to right side of quilt along one edge.
- When you reach the first corner, mark ¹/₄" from corner of quilt top (**Fig. 19**).

Fig. 19

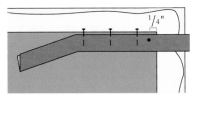

4. Beginning approximately 10" from end of binding and using a ¹/₄" seam allowance, sew binding to quilt, backstitching at beginning of stitching and at mark (**Fig. 20**). Lift needle out of fabric and clip thread.

Fig. 20

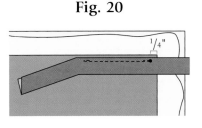

5. Fold binding as shown in **Figs. 21 – 22** and pin binding to adjacent side, matching raw edges. When you reach the next corner, mark ¹/₄" from edge of quilt top.

Fig. 21   **Fig. 22**

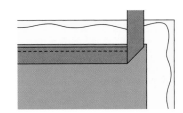

6. Backstitching at edge of quilt top, sew pinned binding to quilt (**Fig. 23**); backstitch when you reach the next mark. Lift needle out of fabric and clip thread.

Fig. 23

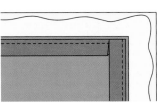

7. Continue sewing binding to quilt, stopping approximately 10" from starting point (**Fig. 24**).

Fig. 24

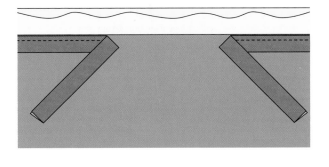

8. Bring beginning and end of binding to center of opening and fold each end back, leaving a ¼" space between folds (**Fig. 25**). Finger-press folds.

Fig. 25

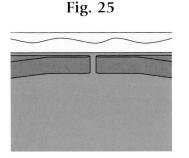

9. Unfold ends of binding and draw a line across wrong side in finger-pressed crease. Draw a line through the lengthwise pressed fold of binding at same spot to create a cross mark. With edge of ruler at cross mark, line up 45° angle marking on ruler with one long side of binding. Draw a diagonal line from edge to edge. Repeat on remaining end, making sure that the two lines are angled the same way (**Fig. 26**).

Fig. 26

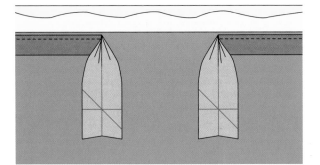

10. Matching right sides and diagonal lines, pin binding ends together at right angles (**Fig. 27**).

Fig. 27

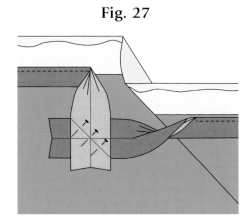

11. Machine stitch along diagonal line, removing pins as you stitch (**Fig. 28**).

Fig. 28

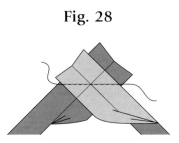

12. Lay binding against quilt to double-check that it is correct length.
13. Trim binding ends, leaving ¼" seam allowance; press seam allowances open. Stitch binding to quilt.
14. Trim backing and batting even with quilt top.
15. On one edge of quilt, fold binding over to quilt backing and pin pressed edge in place, covering stitching line (**Fig. 29**). On adjacent side, fold binding over, forming a mitered corner (**Fig. 30**) Repeat to pin remainder of binding in place.

Fig. 29   **Fig. 30**

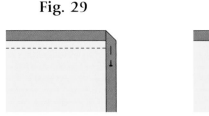

6. Blindstitch binding to backing, taking care not to stitch through to front of quilt. To blindstitch, come up at 1, go down at 2, and come up at 3 (**Fig. 31**). Length of stitches may be varied as desired.

Fig. 31

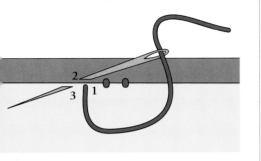

SIGNING AND DATING YOUR QUILT

A completed quilt is a work of art and should be signed and dated. There are many different ways to do this and numerous books on the subject. The label should reflect the style of the quilt, the occasion or person for which it was made, and the quilter's own particular talents. Following are suggestions for recording the history of your quilt or adding a sentiment for future generations.

- Embroider quilter's name, date, and any additional information on quilt top or backing. Matching floss, such as cream floss on a white border, will leave a subtle record. Bright or contrasting floss will make the information stand out.

- Make a label from muslin and use a permanent marker to write information. Use different colored permanent markers to make label more decorative. Stitch label to back of quilt.

- Use photo-transfer paper to add an image to a white or cream fabric label. Stitch label to back of quilt.

- Piece an extra block from quilt top pattern to use as label. Add information with a permanent fabric pen. Appliqué block to back of quilt.

Metric Conversion Chart	
Inches x 2.54 = centimeters (cm)	Yards x .9144 = meters (m)
Inches x 25.4 = millimeters (mm)	Yards x 91.44 = centimeters (cm)
Inches x .0254 = meters (m)	Centimeters x .3937 = inches (")
	Meters x 1.0936 = yards (yd)

Standard Equivalents					
1/8"	3.2 mm	0.32 cm	1/8 yard	11.43 cm	0.11 m
1/4"	6.35 mm	0.635 cm	1/4 yard	22.86 cm	0.23 m
3/8"	9.5 mm	0.95 cm	3/8 yard	34.29 cm	0.34 m
1/2"	12.7 mm	1.27 cm	1/2 yard	45.72 cm	0.46 m
5/8"	15.9 mm	1.59 cm	5/8 yard	57.15 cm	0.57 m
3/4"	19.1 mm	1.91 cm	3/4 yard	68.58 cm	0.69 m
7/8"	22.2 mm	2.22 cm	7/8 yard	80 cm	0.8 m
1"	25.4 mm	2.54 cm	1 yard	91.44 cm	0.91 m

If the magnificent quilts in this collection tempt you to try your hand at designing, you may want to get a dog.

That's right. Miss Rosie of Miss Rosie's Quilt Company is a loveable golden retriever. She's also Carrie Nelson's favorite quilting companion. Miss Rosie gets top billing because she entertains Carrie with her playful antics, adding laughter to each creative day.

"I have to keep the wastebasket out of Rosie's reach," Carrie admits, "or she'll scatter fabric scraps and shred pieces of batting."

One aspect of the business that Miss Rosie doesn't like is when Carrie must travel. Carrie's popularity as a quilting teacher frequently calls her away from home. "If I pack a box to ship, Rosie gets nervous. She thinks I'm going out of town again."

When Carrie isn't leading a quilt class, she's able to set her own work hours, which has helped her to choose a healthy lifestyle. "For about two years now, I've been able to make regular trips to the gym. I do feel better. And people are telling me that I look better. So then, of course, I feel great!"

So how does Miss Rosie like her "new" owner?

"I have more stamina for long walks with Rosie. I'm also able to get down on her level and play, even though we're having triple-digit weather here in Arizona. She's really enjoying that. At this very moment, she's just come indoors to get out of the sun. I believe she wants some ice cubes in her water dish."

When asked if Miss Rosie is perhaps a bit pampered, Carrie laughs, "Miss Rosie, spoiled? Would I spoil my puppy?"

And who can blame Carrie — any dog that can inspire such a winsome brand of quilted artistry should have all the ice she wants, whatever the season.

EDITORIAL STAFF
Vice President and Editor-in-Chief: Sandra Graham Case. *Executive Director of Publications:* Cheryl Nodine Gunnells. *Senior Director of Publications:* Susan White Sullivan. *Director of Designer Relations:* Debra Nettles. *Publications Director:* Cheryl Johnson. *Director of Retail Marketing:* Stephen Wilson. *Art Operations Director:* Jeff Curtis. TECHNICAL — *Technical Editor:* Lisa Lancaster. *Technical Writer:* Frances Huddleston. ART — *Art Publications Director:* Rhonda Hodge Shelby. *Art Imaging Director:* Mark Hawkins. *Art Category Manager:* Lora Puls. *Lead Graphic Artist:* Dayle Carozza. *Graphic Artist:* Stephanie Hamling. *Imaging Technician:* Mark R. Potter. *Photographer:* Lloyd Litsey. *Photography Stylists:* Cassie Francioni and Sondra Daniel. *Publishing Systems Administrator:* Becky Riddle. *Publishing Systems Assistants:* Clint Hanson, Josh Hyatt, and John Rose.

BUSINESS STAFF
Chief Operating Officer: Tom Siebenmorgen. *Vice President, Sales and Marketing:* Pam Stebbins. *Director of Sales and Services:* Margaret Reinold. *Vice President, Operations:* Jim Dittrich. *Comptroller, Operations:* Rob Thieme. *Retail Customer Service Manager:* Stan Raynor. *Print Production Manager:* Fred F. Pruss.

Made in the United States of America.

ISBN 1-57486-536-6

10 9 8 7 6 5 4 3 2

PRINTED WITH SOY INK

Made in U.S.A.